TRANSFORMING DINÉ EDUCATION

TRANSFORMING DINÉ EDUCATION

Innovations in Pedagogy and Practice

Edited by PEDRO VALLEJO and VINCENT WERITO

THE UNIVERSITY OF
ARIZONA PRESS

TUCSON

The University of Arizona Press
www.uapress.arizona.edu

We respectfully acknowledge the University of Arizona is on the land and territories of Indigenous peoples. Today, Arizona is home to twenty-two federally recognized tribes, with Tucson being home to the O'odham and the Yaqui. Committed to diversity and inclusion, the University strives to build sustainable relationships with sovereign Native Nations and Indigenous communities through education offerings, partnerships, and community service.

ISBN-13: 978-0-8165-4354-0 (hardcover)
ISBN-13: 978-0-8165-4353-3 (paperback)

Cover design by Leigh McDonald
Cover image adapted from Meriç Dağlı/Unsplash

Publication of this book is made possible in part by the proceeds of a permanent endowment created with the assistance of a Challenge Grant from the National Endowment for the Humanities, a federal agency.

Library of Congress Cataloging-in-Publication Data
Names: Vallejo, Pedro (Mexican educator) editor. | Werito, Vincent, 1972– editor.
Title: Transforming Diné education : innovations in pedagogy and practice / edited Pedro Vallejo and Vincent Werito.
Description: Tucson : The University of Arizona Press, 2022. | Includes bibliographical references and index.
Identifiers: LCCN 2021042963 | ISBN 9780816543540 (hardcover) | ISBN 9780816543533 (paperback)
Subjects: LCSH: Navajo Indians—Education. | Culturally relevant pedagogy.
Classification: LCC E99.N3 T737 2022 | DDC 979.1004/9726—dc23
LC record available at https://lccn.loc.gov/2021042963

Printed in the United States of America
♾ This paper meets the requirements of ANSI/NISO Z39.48-1992 (Permanence of Paper).

CONTENTS

ACKNOWLEDGMENTS

A S EDITORS of this book, we acknowledge the land (our mother), the sky (our father), and everything in between (that is, all of our relations in the earth below us, in the mountains, in the lifegiving waters, in the air/sky, and all around us). We acknowledge our ancestors who have shared their knowledge with us through stories, as well as our grandparents, our parents, and our extended relatives. We would like to thank both of our families, our children, and our friends for their ongoing support of our work. We are thankful to all of the authors in this book and all of our relatives who will read and take in the knowledge into their lives, their homes, their schools, and their communities and share with others. We would like to thank everyone at the University of Arizona Press for their ongoing support of this work.

TRANSFORMING DINÉ EDUCATION

INTRODUCTION

THE STATE OF NAVAJO EDUCATION

Challenges and Innovations for Diné Education

VINCENT WERITO AND PEDRO VALLEJO

ROM 1864 to 1868, our ancestors were imprisoned at a place they called Hwééldi, or Fort Sumner, New Mexico (Denetdale 2008). In 1868, with the signing of the U.S. Treaty of 1868, the Navajo (Diné) were allowed to return to their traditional homelands. While historians have written that the Diné were released due to the goodwill of the U.S. Peace Commission, Diné perspectives of this historic traumatic event portray a different story—a counter-narrative. According to Diné elders, our ancestors were allowed to return to their homelands because of their continued practice of Diné ceremonies and prayers as well as their spiritual faith (W. Aronilth Jr., pers. comm., June 11, 1998). After four grueling years of confinement, our ancestors' prayers were answered by the Holy People (Diyin Dine'é) and they were allowed to return to their homelands to live and thrive once again.

Over time, despite many hardships they encountered due to American settler/colonial policies, practices, and laws (Dunbar-Ortiz 2014), their land base and population grew significantly, and their livestock expanded to immense numbers as they strived to reclaim their ancestors' ways of life. Due to the trauma of the Long Walk as well as other events to come, like the boarding school experiment of late 1880s, the Spanish Flu epidemic of 1918, and the livestock reduction of the 1930s, the Diné as a people have really never been the same. As a consequence of these events stemming largely from U.S. government policies of cultural genocide and assimilation, many Navajo communities have lost their deep connections to land, age-old ceremonies, and many traditional practices related to birth and burials, and they have slowly become dependent on the U.S. settler/colonialist regime. Consequently, they continue to deal with many social ills brought on by historical/intergenerational trauma and unresolved grief (Alfred 2009; Yellow Horse Brave Heart 1998).

One of the promises made by the U.S. government to our early Navajo leaders in the Navajo Treaty of 1868 (Naaltsoos sání) was a white man's education, including English instruction (Bilagáana bi'oltá dóó bizaad), to improve Navajo lives once they returned to Diné Bikéyah (their homelands). Specifically, the U.S. government promised to provide schools for future generations of Navajo children under Article 6 of the Navajo Treaty of 1868 (Brugge 1965). Similar to many other treaties between the U.S. government and Indian tribes, the particular passage from this treaty article reads:

> To insure the civilization of the Indians entering into this treaty, **the necessity of education is admitted**, especially of such of them as may be settled on said agricultural parts of this reservation, and they therefore **pledge themselves to compel their children**, male and female, between the ages of six and sixteen years, **to attend school**; and it is hereby made the duty of the agent for said Indians to see that this stipulation is strictly complied with; **and the United States agrees** that, for every thirty children between said ages who can be induced or compelled to attend school, **a house shall be provided, and a teacher competent to teach the elementary branches of an English education** shall be furnished, who will reside among said Indians, and faithfully discharge his or her duties as a teacher. (Kappler 1904, 1015–20; emphasis added)

Since this historic signing, schools have become sites of struggle and contestation over maintaining and sustaining Diné culture, identity, language, and a unique way of life.

This chapter provides a brief historical overview of Navajo education and examines the notion of Western education or schooling in contrast to Diné education. Finally, we provide a rationale for the book and an overview of the chapters that highlight transformative teaching practices and educational programs in Diné education.

A BRIEF HISTORY OF NAVAJO EDUCATION

Past attempts to address the "Indian Problem" have advanced in three waves, or progressions, until very recently (Adams 1995; Tyack 2001). They involved efforts associated with (1) removal or extinction, (2) cultural assimilation, and (3) homogenization by promoting a pan-Indian approach. Essentially, the first wave was intended simply to kill off the resistant Indigenous nations or tribes. From the mid-1800s to early 1900s, as many white Americans moved west in search of land or gold, there were increased interactions between Indigenous people and these white settler-colonialists (Dunbar-Ortiz 2014). In response to white settlers' demands for protection against Indian tribes, the U.S. Army engaged in a long war campaign against resistant Indian tribes. By the close of the Indian wars in the late nineteenth century, fewer than 238,000 Indigenous people remained, a sharp decline from the estimated five to fifteen million living in North America when Columbus arrived in 1492 (Fixico 2018). During that time span, multiple wars and diseases took a toll on tribes.

Despite the failed efforts to destroy all remnants of Indigenous people, other motives prevailed, like assimilation instead of all-out genocide (Adams 1995; Dunbar-Ortiz 2014). In response to criticisms of genocide, the U.S. government began efforts to culturally assimilate Indigenous people into white mainstream society instead of eradicating them, first by relocating them onto reservations and then by mandating Western education (Adams 1995). Starting in the late 1880s to mid-1900s, many Native American children (including Navajo) were sent to attend off-reservation boarding schools like the Carlisle Indian Industrial School in Pennsylvania (Adams 1995; Reyhner and Eder 2004) and on-reservation boarding schools like the Ft. Defiance Boarding School in Arizona (Roessel 1977). This began the boarding school experiment that continues into the present day with the idea that "Indian children would have to be removed from the reservation environment altogether if they were going to be effectively assimilated" (Adams 1995, 55).

Reyhner and Eder (1992, 33) write, "Whenever there was close contact between white settlers and Indians, Indians were pressured to conform to white ways of behaving, including the adoption of Christianity, 'civilized dress,' and farming. Education was seen as a way of assimilating young Indians into dominant society." In looking at the history of Indian education, it is also important to see the acts of resistance by Indigenous people to becoming a part of mainstream white society so as not to lose their cultural identity.

In 1928, the Meriam Report was published in an effort to present a nonpolitical investigation into the problem of Indian administration, including education. Problems such as cutting food budgets at boarding schools by 25 percent, general health care for Indian children, lack of relevance in school curriculum to reservation life, not addressing preservice training of teachers of Indian children, and violations of labor laws were all the criticisms of the Indian Bureau overseeing Indians under the Hoover administration (Reyhner and Eder 2004, 208). This report and the subsequent response to improve Indian education led to turning the tide toward improving education for Indigenous people nationally. Among the changes of the federal government was the creation of day schools for Navajo students due to the "still nomadic structure of the sheep-grazing Navajo economy [that] worked against fixed-site day schools" (Reyhner and Eder 2004, 231).

In the later part of the 1800s, as white traders began to set up trading posts in the Southwest and in Navajo country, English became more accessible for communication and trade (Kelley and Francis 2019; Roessel 1977). However, many Navajo communities still lived in isolation from American society well into the 1940s (Young 1961). Despite the U.S. government's efforts and promise to educate Navajo children as stipulated in the treaty of 1868, many were still not in school well into the 1950s. In 1946, in response to the number of Navajo students who had never been inside a schoolhouse despite the promise of the U.S. government, the Indian Bureau developed a Special Navajo Education Program (Thompson 1975). At this time, it was estimated that roughly three-fourths of the entire Navajo children population was still out of school (Roessel 1977; Thompson 1975). Over time, with the advent of a capitalist wage economy that was being imposed on Navajo people (Kelley and Francis 2019), there would be an increase in the creation of more community boarding schools, day schools, and trailer schools in the 1950s and 1960s (Roessel 1977).

In the 1960s, people of color across the United States, including Indigenous communities especially in urban centers, began to push back against inequality and structural inequities (Dunbar-Ortiz 2014). As the civil rights movement gained national attention, Indigenous communities began to assert their rights to self-determination and political sovereignty, especially in education. These initial efforts, starting in the 1950s, led up to the creation of the tribally controlled school movement and the development of Indigenous bilingual education programs (McCarty 2002; Szasz 1999). Over time, the Bureau of Indian Affairs and the Office of Indian Education had more prominent roles in schools. More progress came in the forms of the creation of Navajo Community College (Diné College) and most recently the Navajo Technical University. As the Navajo Nation begins to assume more responsibility for the educational needs of its members by working with public school districts in border towns, parochial schools, and charter schools, their efforts have directly impacted their students by asserting a move toward advancing their own system or model of Diné education.

An important question that we address in this chapter and throughout the book involves distinguishing Indigenous (Diné) perspectives of education from the processes of schooling as characterized in Western education. That is, the first, *Indigenous education*, is different from the mainstream American notions of education as *schooling*. Education from an Indigenous perspective is viewed as a lifelong process, while the process of schooling is viewed as occurring for a short period of time within "a state organized or regulated institution of intentional instruction" (Levinson, Foley, and Holland 1996, 2). Lomawaima and McCarty (2006) make important distinctions between Indigenous education, American Indian education, and schooling. They maintain that American Indian education is the colonial education that was imposed on Indigenous communities through the creation and implementation of Indian boarding schools. More importantly, Lomawaima and McCarty (2006) distinguish between Indigenous education and the process of schooling, where the latter pertains more to what knowledge is deemed most important and how power and privilege operate in schools as institutions through social/cultural reproduction (Apple 2000, 2001a; Bowles

and Gintis [1976] 2011). In contrast, Indigenous education is characterized as the internalization of Indigenous epistemological, "ecological,"
and traditional knowledge acquired through language and social/cultural
practices that are passed on from one generation to the next in Indigenous communities (Cajete 1994; Deloria and Wildcat 2001; Lomawaima
and McCarty 2006).

Bass and Good (2004, 162) state that there are two different Latin
roots for "education": "educare," which means to train and mold, and
"educere," meaning to lead out. Over time, the meanings of these ideas
have changed in terms of how educators frame and talk about education. In comparison to Indigenous perspectives of education, European
perspectives differ in terms of purpose and structure. Thus, generally
speaking, education is viewed as the acquisition of a type of knowledge that is of most worth gained through academics (book knowledge)
and technical skills (writing and reading), often fragmented into areas
of study like math, science, literature, and the humanities. Moreover,
Western education is very Eurocentric in how it promotes its ways of
understanding and viewing the world (i.e., epistemology, ontology, and
philosophy), which is further validated by Western science and Western
religions. Deloria writes:

> Science and Religion are concepts derived wholly from within the Western
> historical experience. They do not appear as separate endeavors in the
> worldviews or experiences of many other cultures. They originate in the
> great synthesis of medieval times when, after the introduction and absorp-
> tion of Aristotelian philosophy of the West, reason and revelation came
> to be regarded as the two equally valid ways of understanding the world,
> indeed of reaching god. (2002, 24)

Thus, education has become a systemized body of Western knowledge
regulated by institutions using systems of archival knowledge that are
constitutive and representative of what it means to be educated in the
right way by earning advanced degrees, instead of an intuitive process of
learning to spur creativity and discovery from within and internalizing
knowledge for life's sake (Apple 2001b; Cajete 1999). In sum, the primary
purpose of schooling vis-à-vis education is to create a society of citizens
who carry on the beliefs and knowledge that reflect the larger system of

knowledge and institutions that perpetuate white, Eurocentric ideals and world perspectives.

Consequently, the attainment of knowledge has become mostly for personal gain and success, measured by academic merits and advanced degrees. Yet, who has access to these bodies of knowledge is predetermined by larger, complex social, political, and economic processes of social and cultural reproduction and racializing institutions that truly do not provide equal opportunity for all, contrary to popular belief about a level playing field (Apple 2000, 2001b; Bowles and Gintis 2011; Lewis 2005). Further, Western approaches to education essentially are predicated on instilling and promoting fundamental aspects of capitalism, patriarchy, and white supremacy in their specific use of terms like "academic achievement" and "Common Core knowledge," as well as on white nationalistic goals of keeping America great and spreading freedom and democracy around the world. Thus, the Western approach to education has impacted American society in two ways: "By teaching correct political principles to the young, they could nurture virtuous citizens. Equally important, local control gave adult citizens a chance to exercise self-rule" (Tyack 2001, 1). The concern with this approach has been that minorities and marginalized groups continue to be excluded from either action. The national definition of "virtuous citizens" did not include people of color. Self-rule, which can be understood as self-determination, has also been impacted. For tribes across the United States, self-determination has always been central and important to their continued existence. Thus, the definition of "virtuous citizens" is conditional and excluded Indigenous peoples. True self-determination, or sovereignty, for Indigenous nations could weaken the power of the U.S. government, which it has not truly allowed in education or elsewhere (Lomawaima and McCarty 2006).

OVERVIEW OF THE BOOK

This book presents examples of Diné-centered educational models and aspects of Diné pedagogy through stories about Diné resilience, resistance, and survival that lie at the core of our unique worldview and goal to always strive to overcome life's obstacles and achieve long life in happiness. Obviously, the pursuit of knowledge for personal economic motives stands in contrast to Diné epistemologies and perspectives about how one acquires knowledge, for what purpose, and what its outcomes may be. As such, this book offers a Diné perspective of education honoring and recognizing the work of these educators in the areas of culture-based education, special education, language revitalization, wellness, tribal sovereignty and self-determination in education, and university/tribal/community partnerships. The collected contributions of the authors in this book represent only a fraction of existing programs for our Diné youth and nation.

For this book, we chose Diné educators who are using aspects of their Diné cultural knowledge, language, and cultural paradigms to advance Navajo education. In particular, the chapters in this book share stories and unique perspectives of Diné and non-Diné educators that lay the foundation for advancing a Diné-centered pedagogy for transformative educational praxis that is much needed today. The work behind this project has been an endeavor for the past five years. In developing and planning for this project, our initial discussions were about clarifying our goal for documenting an emerging educational direction in Diné education. We noted that in recent years, there has been a strengthening and renewed sense of self-determination to reclaim our culture and our language among many educators of Diné youth. With this in mind, we wanted to know how we could best present the work of the practitioners, schools, and different programs in Diné education for our Diné youth that is created by Diné educators with a Diné cultural perspective. In short, we wanted a book about Diné education that comes directly from the source, the land, and from Diné communities. This book is the result of those discussions.

This was a journey that we knew could not be made alone. We needed the experience and knowledge of others who were in the middle of making changes. We shared the idea with many Diné educators we knew who are on the forefront of advancing Diné pedagogical programs in various educational institutions in and around Diné Bikéyah and the states surrounding the reservation. Diné Bikéyah includes parts of New Mexico, Arizona, and Utah that the Navajo Nation covers. Some of our invited guests were already involved with other projects and were unable to participate. We are thankful for the contributing authors of this book who were able to provide a chapter. We are grateful they are sharing their experiences in Diné education.

Part I specifically focuses on K–12 programs and classrooms. Part II has topics related to the educational programs that influence K–12 education, including discussions on teacher preparation, what it means to be educated as Diné, and the significance of a Diné wellness approach to education. Part III focuses on Diné educational sovereignty and articulating a Diné-centered pedagogy for transformative educational praxis.

By no means is this book meant to be the definitive word on Diné education. There are other programs we were not able to include but are just as important. Some programs are just now being developed and will take time to come to fruition. Collectively, they define a movement that is just getting started. This book does, however, showcase some of the exciting innovations being made by Diné educators as they continue to move toward educating our youth in a way that allows them to truly know who they are, where they come from, and where they want to go in the future. This positively impacts their communities as they see how their Diné perspectives are an asset to living according to the principles of Hózhǫ́ (the Diné way of living to ensure balance and harmony among and with all things) and to sustain the cultural spiritual practices of K'é (the Diné way of how we relate to each other through familial and tribal ties, including clans) to improve their lives and the lives of those around them. In this way, we ensure our Diné way of knowing, living, and learning continues on.

The authors in this book provide insights about the state of education regarding how they acknowledged the struggles of their ancestors to face their own adversities; how they realized their physical, common, and spiritual image (Aronilth 1992, 1994) and cultural strengths to overcome challenges; and how they drew on their wisdom/knowledge from within to achieve harmony and balance in their personal lives, families, and careers along with their community lives and to truly believe in themselves and Diné education for long-term harmonious outcomes and the benefit of future generations. In looking ahead to the possibilities and promises of realizing our ancestors' prayers for continuance of our Diné ways of life for our children, the authors are re-envisioning the promise of Diné education as a decolonizing, transformative educational agenda that moves us toward a Diné-centered politics and pedagogy to restore our humanity, way of life, language, and identity.

REFERENCES CITED

Adams, D. W. 1995. *Education for Extinction: American Indians and the Boarding School Experiences, 1875–1928.* Lawrence: University of Kansas Press.

Alfred, G. T. 2009. "Colonialism and State Dependency." *Journal of Aboriginal Health* 5 (2): 42–60.

Apple, M. 2000. *Official Knowledge: Democratic Education in a Conservative Age.* 2nd ed. New York: Routledge.

Apple, M. 2001a. *Ideology and Curriculum.* 3rd ed. New York: RoutledgeFalmer.

Apple, M. 2001b. *Educating the Right Way: Markets, Standards, God, and Inequality.* New York: RoutledgeFalmer.

Aronilth, W., Jr. 1992. *Foundation of Navajo Culture.* Tsaile, AZ: Diné College.

Aronilth, W., Jr. 1994. *Diné Bi Bee Óhoo'aah Bá Silá: An Introduction to Navajo Philosophy.* 4th ed. Tsaile, AZ: Diné College.

Bass, R., and J. W. Good. 2004. "Educare and Educere: Is a Balance Possible in the Educational System?" *Educational Forum* 68 (2): 161–68.

Bowles, S., and H. Gintis. (1976) 2011. *Schooling in Capitalist America: Educational Reform and the Contradictions of Economic Life.* Chicago: Haymarket Books.

Brugge, D. M. 1965. *Long Ago in Navajoland.* Window Rock, AZ: Navajo Publications.

Cajete, G. 1994. *Look to the Mountain: An Ecology of Indigenous Education.* Denver, CO: Kivakí Press.

Cajete, G. 1999. *Igniting the Sparkle: An Indigenous Science Education Model.* Denver, CO: Kivakí Press.

Deloria, V., Jr., and D. Wildcat. 2001. *Power and Place: Indian Education in America.* Golden, CO: Fulcrum Resources.

Denetdale, J. 2008. *The Long Walk: The Forced Navajo Exile.* New York: Chelsea House.

Dunbar-Ortiz, R. 2014. *An Indigenous People's History of the United States.* Boston: Beacon Press.

Fixico, D. 2018. "When Native Americans Were Slaughtered in the Name of 'Civilization.'" *History.com*, March 2. https://www.history.com/news/native-americans -genocide-united-states.

Kappler, C. J. 1904. *Indian Affairs: Vol. II: Laws and Treaties.* Washington, D.C.: Government Printing Office. https://americanindian.si.edu/static/nationtonation/ pdf/Navajo-Treaty-1868.pdf.

Kelley, K., and H. Francis. 2019. *A Diné History of Navajoland.* Tucson: University of Arizona Press.

Levinson, B., D. Foley, and D. Holland, eds. 1996. *The Cultural Reproduction of the Educated Person: Critical Ethnographies of Schooling and Local Practice.* Albany: State University of New York Press.

Lewis, A. 2005. *Race in the Schoolyard: Negotiating the Color Line in Classrooms and Communities.* New Brunswick, NJ: Rutgers University Press.

Lomawaima, K. T., and T. L. McCarty. 2006. *"To Remain an Indian": Lessons in Democracy from a Century of Native American Education.* New York: Teachers College Press.

McCarty, T. 2002. *A Place to Be Navajo: Rough Rock and the Struggle for Self-Determination in Indigenous Schooling.* Mahwah, NJ: Lawrence-Erlbaum.

Reyhner, J., and J. Eder. 1992. *A History of Indian Education.* Billings, MT: Council for Indian Education.

Reyhner, J., and J. Eder. 2004. *American Indian Education: A History.* Norman: University of Oklahoma Press.

Szasz, M. C. 1999. *Education and the American Indian: The Road to Self-Determination, 1928–1998.* Albuquerque: University of New Mexico Press.

Roessel, R. A., and Navaho Curriculum Center. 1977. *Navajo Education in Action: The Rough Rock Demonstration School.* Chinle, AZ: Navajo Curriculum Center, Rough Rock Demonstration School.

Thompson, H. 1975. *The Navajos' Long Walk for Education: A History of Navajo Education.* Tsaile, AZ: Navajo Community College Press.

Tyack, D. 2001. "Introduction." In *School: The Story of American Public Education,* edited by S. Mondale and S. B. Patton, 1–8. Boston: Beacon Press.

Yellow Horse Brave Heart, M. 1998. "The Return to the Sacred Path: Healing the Historical Trauma and Historical Unresolved Grief Response among the Lakota." *Smith College Studies in Social Work* 68 (3): 287–305.

Young, R. 1961. *The Navajo Yearbook.* Window Rock, AZ: Bureau of Indian Affairs, Navajo Agency.

PART I

SCHOOL SITE AND COMMUNITY-BASED PROGRAMS

Culture-Based Math Programs, Special Education,
Language Revitalization, and Wellness

CHAPTER 1

MULTICULTURAL EDUCATION

Navajo Culturally Relevant Mathematics Education

HENRY FOWLER

THE UNITED STATES is becoming more diversified. The large number of "old immigrants" from Europe is now being replaced by a new wave of immigrants from Asia, Central America, Mexico, India, and Somalia (Nelson, Palonsky, and McCarthy 2013). In 2050, the white population will grow slightly and will eventually become a minority, while the Latino population will triple in size, and other immigrants will continue to increase in number. According to Nelson, Palonsky, and McCarthy (2013), the number of immigrants born overseas will rapidly increase in the United States, which will create a tapestry of America that will be more diversified than its current state. Multicultural education in the twenty-first century cannot be ignored. This chapter will examine different forms of multicultural education definitions, pros and cons about multicultural education, and recommended actions on multicultural education.

DEFINITIONS OF MULTICULTURAL EDUCATION

In order to create a classroom that accommodates all learners and prepares them for a diverse society, Nelson, Palonsky, and McCarthy (2013) and Gay (2000) explain that there are different definitions of multicultural education. They describe multicultural education as a concept of culture, and they examine culture as problems arise from cultural conflicts. In this perspective, scholars in the field argue that students should understand the conflicting teaching and knowledge demands between home and school cultures. Nelson, Palonsky, and McCarthy (2013) noted that students should also understand different cultural conflicts between the powerless and the powerful, as well as unequal treatment of people because of race, ethnicity, gender, and sexual orientation. Other scholars have defined multicultural education based on agents of change. This approach encourages reforming the society with political and ethical behavior to assist the disadvantaged and non-white to perform well and make gains in social and economic circles.

In addition to these multicultural education definitions, other multiculturalists have challenged the "Eurocentric" methods of confining their approaches in school curricula ranging from knowledge construction, to individualism, to empirical data (Nelson, Palonsky, and McCarthy 2013, 261). The National Association for Multicultural Education (2003) defined multicultural education as an educational process that integrates all aspects of school policies and practices. It provides a framework for students to participate actively and pursue structural equality in organizations by providing them with knowledge and skills to improve society. Nelson, Palonsky, and McCarthy (2013) indicated that students can improve society through multicultural education by eradicating racism, classism, heterosexism, and religious intolerance. Nieto and Bode (2008) add that multicultural education is about social justice and strategies to confront educational equality. Multicultural education offers students the opportunity to appreciate their own positive aspects, which leads them to respect each other and be sensitive to each other's cultural backgrounds.

The conservative side of multicultural education is "we are all multiculturalists." Whether you oppose it or like it, multicultural education is here to stay and is unavoidable (Glazer 1997, 147). America is uniquely composed of many diverse cultural groups. The non-white students have a right to belong to any area of learning taught in school, since America was created from many diverse backgrounds, contributions, and perspectives. According to Banks and McGee Banks (2007), to implement successful multicultural education, schools must recognize the various dimensions of multicultural education. Nelson, Palonsky, and McCarthy (2013) mention that multicultural education needs to be defined from broad perspectives so that school disciplines and staff can implement an appropriate multicultural education model.

GOALS OF MULTICULTURAL EDUCATION

Multicultural education advocates pluralism and is in line with freedom based on a democratic society where everyone has equal rights and is treated equally. Multicultural education launched its goals based on this perspective. Nelson, Palonsky, and McCarthy (2013) suggested four goals of multicultural education: (1) individuals are respected and valued, (2) acknowledgment and understanding of diverse perspectives, (3) school curriculum is meaningful and relevant, and (4) opportunities for all students.

Everyone has a meaningful hue in the web of life. Each hue is symbolic of how people learn and construct knowledge. The multiple waves of colors represent different backgrounds of people in how they understand different phenomena based on their schemata of lenses. Every color of light adds warmness to a space; similarly, every color of human should be cherished, valued, and respected. Nelson, Palonsky, and McCarthy (2013, 263) indicate that "everyone develops separate frames of reference for interpreting the social and political world." Multicultural education supports and nurtures respect for all cultural groups of people (Nelson, Palonsky, and McCarthy 2013).

All groups have a rich culture, heritage, and traditions. The American way of life integrates different perspectives of people from different parts of the world. According to Nelson, Palonsky, and McCarthy (2013), there is no knowledge that is more superior or genuine than others; the knowledge of all people deserves appreciation. Banks (2002) reminds us that people of color's knowledge about their way of life is not recognized in Western culture as true human experience. Nelson, Palonsky, and McCarthy (2013) point out that schools are obligated to acknowledge multiple perspectives in curricula and teach diversity as a means to reduce prejudice and racism and argue that "viewing any event from diverse, competing viewpoints leads to a fuller, more complete representation of truth" (2013, 265). Schools need to consider and reflect the truth of cultural diversity in what the students are learning. For example, according to Nelson, Palonsky, and McCarthy (2013), children who are immigrants from Asia, India, Latin America, and other places need to understand the ancestral lands that they left and their rich cultural history.

Another goal of multicultural education is to create a school curriculum around the learners so that the lessons are meaningful, engaging, and relevant to all (Nelson, Palonsky, and McCarthy 2013). Nelson, Palonsky, and McCarthy (2013) and Banks (2002) explain that school curricula have more meaning for students when students can relate to the characters in the stories they read, and instruction is appealing to the students when the lessons reflect their experiences and prior knowledge.

Multicultural education calls for fairness and justice for all students. For so long, schools have done a disservice to students of color by teaching them about Western knowledge only while ignoring the students' cultural learning and practices (Nelson, Palonsky, and McCarthy 2013). Multicultural education calls for a fair share of school curricula and honest representations and treatments of all learners.

OPPOSITION TO MULTICULTURAL EDUCATION

Those who oppose multicultural education argue that it is destroying Western civilization. Huntington (1996) chastises multicultural education as a means of tearing apart America's sense of identity and patriotism, arguing that the multiculturalists have "denied the existence of a common American culture" (305). Hirsch (2006) argues that the nation would collapse under the ideology of multicultural education, and to prevent this from happening, the country needs to adopt a common curriculum for all students to study. Bloom (1987) adds that all cultural epistemologies have equal value, and this would apparently contribute toward destroying traditional Western culture and values. Ravitch (2003) mentions that multicultural education would darken American schools and disperse American society. Huntington (1996) and Hirsch (2006) view American society as possessing a white, male, Western orientation. Hirsch (2006) notes that all newcomers should be influenced and indoctrinated by the "American" society. The call of Hirsch is evident in formal mainstream education. For example, the report "A Curriculum of Inclusion" in the 1980s showed that New York's school curriculum was not recognizing minorities' ways of life, and this finding is parallel to many other states where Western education does not acknowledge other ways of life (Nelson, Palonsky, and McCarthy 2013). This model is an example of assimilation into the dominant way of life.

As Native Americans, we continue to struggle with our cultural identities because our way of knowledge is viewed by the Western culture as destructive, contributing to the process of destroying Western civilization (Nelson, Palonsky, and McCarthy 2013). In my view, the common values approach to education is contributing to Native people's hardship; plus, it is contributing to their language loss. The loss of the Navajo language is currently devastating Navajo communities. It is sad to see Navajo children speaking only English in stores, schools, and everywhere on the Navajo Nation. As Navajo educators, it is our responsibility to reinforce the Navajo language in schools.

SUPPORT FOR MULTICULTURAL EDUCATION

Multiculturalists are in favor of multicultural education and argue that all learners can succeed in life no matter what their cultural values and practices are. Students who see their culture in the school curriculum find success in school. The multiculturalists support schools in teaching multiple cultural perspectives to account for academic equality, fairness, and accurate historical developments (Nelson, Palonsky, and McCarthy 2013). Multicultural education encourages the use of cultural tales of the disadvantaged and the marginalized in mainstream school curricula. The advantages of multicultural education are that it teaches respect for all cultural diversity and embraces people from different cultural backgrounds. Reducing prejudice, decreasing racism, and fostering interaction between cultural groups are the most important aspects of multicultural education (Nelson, Palonsky, and McCarthy 2013).

RECOMMENDED ACTIONS

Just as the description and principles of multicultural education imply, curricula transformations for students of color should involve the inclusion of their culture, experiences, and learning styles. Teaching techniques should be appropriate to students' learning styles, and instructional materials should support students' cultural qualities (Banks 2002). Teaching only mainstream ideology and culture deprives students of learning from the rich experiences of other ethnicities and colors (Banks 2002). Multicultural education calls for a curriculum transformation that considers attitude and behavior changes in working with students of color. As an educator, I believe it is time to consider the goals of multicultural education for students' mathematics education in the Navajo Nation. For so many years, their formal education has been based on a Western culture. My recommendation is to ponder the position of the multicultural approach in developing curriculum for Navajo students, particularly in mathematics.

The Navajo Cultural Component Math Curriculum (NCCMC) is a math supplementary curriculum for mainstream mathematics education. The aim of the NCCMC is to assist the mainstream math curriculum in helping Navajo students understand mathematical concepts. Around the globe, people have invented math according to their needs, and the Navajo people are no exception. Here, I will use the recommended role of the dimensions of multicultural education to demonstrate that math concepts can be taught using Navajo epistemology. The dimensions of multicultural education are as follows:

1. Content Integration: teachers use a variety of disciplines and cultures in teaching academic subjects.
2. Equity Pedagogy: teachers plan lessons that encourage success of students that come from diverse cultural backgrounds.
3. Knowledge Construction Process: teachers help students understand how academic content can relate to their cultural practices and values.
4. Prejudice Reduction: teachers plan lessons that will change students' feelings toward other groups of students.
5. Empowering School Culture and Social Structure: the school culture acknowledges and empowers different cultural groups in school operations. (Nelson, Palonsky, and McCarthy 2013)

The multicultural-approach lesson is designed to engage students in thinking about the math concept in relation to one of the most universal symbols for the Navajo, the hogan. The Navajo way of life depends on *hózhǫ́*, or balance and order, to maintain a good life with the natural order of the universe. This parallel relationship with the natural order of the universe allows the students to think about order as it relates to the order of evaluating numerical expressions.

Teaching for understanding is a vital aspect of mathematical learning. This lesson engages students in the order of operations using the Navajo perspective of orderliness respective to the social order of their traditional home, the hogan.

ORDER OF OPERATIONS

A hogan (in Navajo, hooghan) is a traditional circular-shaped house still used by Navajos. The hogan is more than just a place to eat and sleep. It is the core of Navajo life. It is the foundation of concepts and values of tradition, culture, and philosophy of the Navajo people. The hogan is the center of the orderly process of life for a Navajo. Inside the hogan, the order of process of motion is clockwise, or left to right. In this essence of whirling spiral of Navajo teaching, traditional teaching methods are still vital to Navajo family organization. Navajos use their hogans as the starting point for instruction for the young and as the primary bridge to other aspects of their children's experience. Navajo elder Sally Fowler (pers. comm., February 4, 2017) said, "Life begins in the hogan; from there, circling around to great distances in an ever-widening circle to broader, more complex realities, such as Kinaaldá [coming-of-age ritual for girls], rituals, ceremonies, adulthood, and parenthood." The hogan does not just provide shelter. It is also the actual location where such values are traditionally transmitted from generation to generation, and it serves as a symbol for ideal thought and action. The family hogan is the center of the beginning and order of the operation of life. A child is taught that the hogan lies at life's core. Therefore, at birth, the Navajo child's head is turned toward the hogan fire so that the soft spot on top of the child's head is heated and properly shaped. Proper shaping includes correct thought as well as good behavior. The child is taught the proper order of balance and harmony through k'é. K'é is the proper order of respect through a balanced and harmonious relationship with all the elements of the environment. In a hogan, the proper order of k'é, or respect, is based on the expansion of positive energy movement in a clockwise, or left to right, motion around the hogan's fire.

The hogan fire, situated at the center of the hogan's interior, becomes the warm, inviting spot where parents and grandparents recite stories and share the comforting support of their own life experience with children as they grow and develop. Performing household chores and caring for items inside and related to the hogan furnish children's first lessons in adult responsibility. This lesson provides the proper order of evaluating numerical expressions just like the order of teaching from the Navajo hogan.

Based on Navajo teachings, the hogan is made of four orders of natural elements: to the east is the White Shell, to the south is the Turquoise, to the west is the Abalone Shell, and to the north is the Black Jet. This model will use the directional perspective of order associated with the four cardinal directions to accentuate learning of the order of operations.

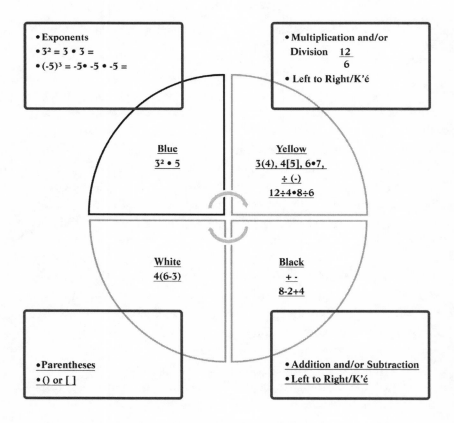

FIGURE 1.1 Navajo philosophy and order of operations.

HOGAN COLORS:

- This circle represents a hogan. The proper way of greeting or moving in a hogan is from left to right starting from the entrance. The colors mark different times of the day. White represents early dawn, blue represents midday, yellow represents the sunset, and black represents darkness; these colors are folded to make a hogan.
- The order of operations represents a numerical value. To find the numerical value, the rules for order of operations are used to determine the correct answer. Use the hogan colors to solve the order of operations.
- White represents doing all the operations within the parentheses and brackets. Blue represents working on all the exponents. Yellow represents doing all the operations of multiplication and division as they occur from left to right. Black represents doing all the operations of addition and subtraction as they occur from left to right.

For example, this is how to use order of operations of the hogan colors: $2^3 \cdot -5 + 4(-2)$.

WHITE/BLUE/YELLOW/BLACK

1. The early dawn brings new purpose in life. Following the hogan color model, operations inside the parentheses are done first. Early light greets 6−8 (white). The early dawn presents this new expression as $2^3 \cdot -5 + 4(-2)$.
2. Next, the blue color represents exponents, or daylight. The daylight greets 2 to the third power. The daylight creates this expression: $8 \cdot -5 + 4(-2)$.
3. The yellow color represents multiplication and division and sunset. Perform the operation from left to right. The hogan color models this relationship. The motion in a hogan is left to right, and greeting people in a hogan is left to right. Do the multiplication next. The sunset, or the yellow color, presents a new expression to simplify, $-40 + -8$.
4. The black color represents addition, subtraction, and darkness. Darkness is presented in the final computation, which results in -40.

This model enables the students to see the problem as a whole and relates the students to the order of operations for life based on their cultural teachings. In Navajo teaching, our life is dictated by the movement and energy of the sun. This model captures that energy in teaching order of operations. The experience of math in a cultural context illustrates how mathematical ideas are interrelated to produce a coherent whole.

NAVAJO SYSTEMS OF EDUCATION

I recollect my way of life by coming home to my home fire. My ancestors orally told me that our home fire is sacred, sacred because the fire is a representation of our ancestors who had embraced the richness of the Navajo way of life. The Navajo way of life has framed my perspective and my ways of knowing through my environment. It was my mother who introduced me to understanding myself through her subtle, keen understanding of herself as a Navajo woman. My mother has no formal Western education. Her sense of knowing is strongly tied to the philosophy and spirituality of the Mother Earth, Father Sky, and Mother Nature. My mother's name is Sally Fowler. Her ways of communicating are through her breadth of knowledge based on the Navajo people. The Navajo people have had an education system in place since the beginning of time. That system is woven in songs, prayers, ceremonies, and oral storytelling of the Navajo Creation Story, which frames Navajo epistemology. In this way, Navajo epistemology comes from the womb of Mother Earth, Father Sky, sacred mountains, darkness and day, white and yellow corn, Corn Pollen Boy, Beetle Girl, Changing Woman, First Man and Woman, fire, water, and air.

Senge et al. (1994) defined systems thinking as the interrelated whole of elements wherein the elements have a common pattern that works together toward a common purpose. Capra (1996) described systems thinking in the milieu as connection, relationship, and association. Capra also implied that systems thinking was related to living organisms and social systems. In my background, Navajos view the world as a living system and have a relational connection to it as follows: Earth is "Mother Earth," the sky is "Father Sky," darkness is "Grandparents," and the sun is "Father." According to Fowler (pers. comm., February 4, 2017), the Navajo believe they are in balance and in harmony with the natural order of the universe through these elements. For example, the Navajo face their home in the direction of the east to greet the first sunlight. The first sunlight symbolizes a new beginning that is touched with a beauty from the order of the natural element.

Navajos touch the first sun ray to bless themselves and call on it for the well-being of oneself, home, family, all life, and the entire universe. Navajos view every aspect of life as a whole and themselves as an integral part of that whole. Life includes tiny insects, rivers, trees, mountains, and canyons—all of which are included in the elements that complete the natural order of the universe. For Navajos, this phenomenon is an integral part of their life. Fowler (pers. comm., February 4, 2017) stated that if one element does not exist, then there is no life. Furthermore, she postulates the Earth is a living being and a living spirit. Capra (1996) explained this phenomenon as systems thinking, which is characterized as a whole made up of elements derived by the relationship of its parts. This is also the Navajo way.

Navajos believe that their cultural teaching is embedded in the male-female dualism guided by the Protection Way and Blessing Way of teaching. These teachings frame the underlying educational models of knowing. Protection Way teachings safeguard one against the possible problems of life, corruption, and immorality. They help an individual cope with life's hardships and problems. Blessing Way teachings help the individual fulfill a moral life and stay on the footpath of harmony and balance. A balanced life is the state of hózhǫ́, bringing female and male teachings together and complementing all of life around us. These teachings give us the Navajo life standards for walking in beauty and harmony with the world order.

The Navajo believe they are part of nature, and that this natural order gives directions for life. They agree their natural surroundings bring the energy of spirit to the people. That energy is infused with purpose and direction for the Navajo people. According to hózhǫ́, the Navajo purpose on this earth is to keep in balance, harmony, and respect with the natural order. A good life resides in every angle of the morning light with a promising sense of beauty, hope, and determination for every individual. Navajos understand that with a sense of the complementary and supplementary, an individual will feel beauty above, below, around, and before him or her from every angle. We continue to practice this traditional heritage.

- Beauty Before Me: Planning short- and long-term goals for the journey of life.
- Beauty Behind Me: Connecting home and self-identity through k'é (principles to guide all behavior, interactions, and relationships between Navajo people and all things in life).
- Beauty Below Me: Connecting with Mother Earth in relation to Navajo and Western knowledge.
- Beauty Above Me: Connecting with Father Sky in relation to Navajo and Western knowledge.
- Beauty All Around Me: Connecting with the environment and universe in relation to Navajo and Western knowledge.
- With Beauty I Speak: Integrating Navajo and Western knowledge sources. "Through these teachings, I am Sa'ah Naagháí Bik'eh Hózhǫ́ǫ́n. I will have knowledge, k'é, balance, and strength" (S. Fowler, pers. comm., February 4, 2017).
- Based on the fundamental teachings of the Navajo people, Sa'ah Naagháí Bik'eh Hózhǫ́ǫ́n involves the four cardinal directions that reflect the four stages of the life cycle and serve as a means for internalizing knowledge. The internalization process of knowledge becomes the core of one's life. The life principles include:
  - Nitsáhákees (Critical Thinking)
  - Nahat'á (Planning)
  - Iiná (Implementation)
  - Sihasin (Reflection and Assurance)
  - Sa'ah Naagháí Bik'eh Hózhǫ́ǫ́n guides the Navajo principles and values.

CONCLUSION

Multicultural education brought about a reform in education that addressed the inequality in schools that particularly affected children of color who were economically depressed, limited English-speaking, gender irresolute, and disabled. Multicultural education offers a direction to change the structure of education so that all students have equal access to education. Equal access offers a new direction for the Navajo schools to reform their educational practices to support their home cultural identity.

A new direction for math education is vital for Native American and Alaskan Indians, particularly Navajo students, in order for them to successfully integrate themselves into the modern technological world. Culturally relevant math education is a crucial conduit through which adequate and directed access to math education can be imparted. Educators can use their historical and traditional knowledge foundations to build culturally enriched math curricula. These curricula will foster student ability to solve math problems and to communicate and understand mathematical reasoning. The bridge between Navajo culture and school culture will allow Navajo students to fully participate in a math classroom and to make connections to the math content representations. The implementation of the Navajo culturally based math curriculum will assist students in appreciating the role of their native culture in the context of math and to make the math connections that can result in math excellence and proficiency on math standard exams.

REFERENCES CITED

Banks, J. A. 2002. *An Introduction to Multicultural Education*. 3rd ed. Boston: Allyn and Bacon.

Banks, J. A., and C. A. McGee Banks. 2007. *Multicultural Education: Issues and Perspectives* 6th ed. Hoboken, NJ: Wiley.

Bloom, A. 1987. *The Closing of the American Mind: How Higher Education Has Failed Democracy and Impoverished the Souls of Today's Students*. New York: Simon and Schuster.

Capra, F. 1996. *The Web of Life: A New Scientific Understanding of Living Systems*. New York: Anchor Books.

Gay, G. 2000. "The Importance of Multicultural Education." *Educational Leadership* 61 (4): 30–35.

Glazer, N. 1997. *We Are All Multiculturalists Now*. Cambridge, MA: Harvard University Press.

Hirsch, E. D. 2006. *The Knowledge Deficit: Closing the Shocking Education Gap for American Children*. New York: Houghton Mifflin.

Huntington, S. P. 1996. *The Clash of Civilizations: Remaking of the World Order*. New York: Touchstone.

National Association for Multicultural Education. 2003. Resolutions and Position Papers. http://www.nameorg.org/resolutions/definition.html, accessed April 11, 2005.

Nelson, J. L., S. Palonsky, and R. M. McCarthy. 2013. *Critical Issues in Education: Dialogues and Dialectics.* New York: McGraw-Hill.

Nieto, S., and P. Bode. 2008. *Affirming Diversity: The Sociopolitical Context of Multicultural Education.* 5th ed. New York: Pearson.

Ravitch, D. 2003. *The Language Police: How Pressure Groups Restrict What Students Learn.* New York: Alfred A. Knopf.

Senge, P. M., A. Kleiner, C. Roberts, R. B. Ross, and B. J. Smith, B. J. 1994. *The Fifth Discipline Fieldbook: Strategies and Tools for Building a Learning Organization.* New York: Doubleday.

CHAPTER 2

LANGUAGE ASSESSMENT OF NAVAJO CHILDREN

Implications for Research and Practice

CHRISTINE B. VINING AND DAVIS E. HENDERSON

EXAMINING LANGUAGE assessment practices of Navajo children is central to appropriate implementation of Diné special education. Assessing culturally and linguistically diverse children for special education eligibility and overrepresentation of these students in special education have been a concern of educators, special educators, and related service personnel such as speech-language pathologists (SLPs) for decades (Artiles and Ortiz 2002; Artiles and Trent 1994). In the field of speech-language pathology, Bayles and Harris (1982) initially questioned the use of normed referenced speech and language tests for diagnosing American Indian (AI) children in the Southwest. The practice of using standardized tests to determine language disorders in AI children continues despite reported biases inherent in tools not normed on AI populations (Failing, Stice, and Inglebret 1993). As a Navajo bilingual SLP, the first author has long advocated for consideration of cultural variables and language characteristics when assessing AI children, specifically Navajo children (Allison and Vining 1999; Long and Vining 2000; Vining 1997; Westby and Vining 2002). In recent years, Navajo and other AI SLPs began to address some of the long-standing issues related to testing of Navajo children, including dual language learners, to determine whether they meet the requirement for special education and related services such as speech and language impairment (Henderson and Restrepo 2016; Vining et al. 2017). The second author has made significant contributions in his research on how Navajo students perform on standardized language assessment tests (Henderson and Restrepo 2016, 2017; Henderson, Restrepo, and Aiken 2018). In this chapter, we highlight important issues in educational achievement of AI students, the use of standardized testing with Navajo children, and overrepresentation of AI children in special education. We describe current challenges in language assessment of Navajo children to highlight recent research in the use of standardized testing with Navajo students for identification of language delays and disorders and to discuss the implications of current research to improve assessment practices.

EDUCATIONAL ISSUES

In this section, we discuss the historical and current status of AI achievement in New Mexico based on reports by the New Mexico Public Education Department (NMPED). These reports highlight the struggles AI students have with language-based skills such as oral language comprehension and expression, language arts, reading, and writing that support students in becoming literate in English. Our purpose for describing academic achievement for AI students is to illustrate the sizeable gaps in achievement across content areas based on race/ethnicity, income levels, disability status, and English language learner (ELL) status. We also take the stance that students lacking adequate educational experiences and appropriate cultural and linguistic support require systemic aid that does not necessarily warrant a special education referral.

ACHIEVEMENT GAP

Student Achievement in New Mexico

As a state, New Mexico endeavors to meet the academic and cultural needs of its AI students. The *Tribal Education Status Report School Year 2017–18* (TESR; NMPED 2018) indicated that New Mexico Indian education includes twenty-three school districts and six charter schools that serve approximately thirty-four thousand AI students in public schools and six thousand students in the Bureau of Indian Education (BIE)–operated and tribally controlled schools, and that approximately 2.5 percent of staff statewide are AI. Navajo students make up a sizeable representation in this student population. It is also important to note that many of these districts and schools are on or near AI reservations and in rural counties where transportation of students, access to technology, and instruction by highly qualified staff pose educational challenges. Many AI children in these schools are also economically disadvantaged. For example, 41 percent of AI children in New Mexico were living in poverty in 2018; and McKinley County, where there is a large population of Navajo children, had the highest rate with 46 percent of children living in poverty (New Mexico Voices for Children 2019). The AI student population is diverse, and many maintain connections to their Native cultures and languages. The well-being of Navajo and other AI children contributes to how well they are doing academically across the state. Developing and evaluating standards-based assessments allows districts and schools to monitor educational progress.

The TESR report provided results on NMPED (2018) assessment of students in areas of reading for students in K–2 grades, English language arts (grades 3–11), and math (grades 3–11) for the 2017–18 school year (SY). Analysis of the data showed that 29 percent of AI students were proficient in reading, 12 percent in math, and 21 percent in science, which were the lowest proficiency rates in comparison to other racial/ethnic groups. These rates indicate that high percentages of AI children are not passing reading, math, or science assessments and are not making significant progress academically. Based on 2018 test results, academic progress in comparison to assessments in SY 2015–16 showed slight gains (2 percent) in reading and math, and a decrease (1 percent) in science. While the data are not presented by tribe, Navajo students are included in the large majority of AI students who are struggling with math, science, and reading.

In addition, NMPED (2018) compared the 2017–18 statewide assessment proficiencies by economic status, gender, and disability. The report's conclusion that children living in poverty underperformed academically was not surprising. NMPED reported that AI students who were not economically disadvantaged had higher proficiencies across reading, math, and science than AI students who were economically disadvantaged.

These results suggest the impact of poverty on limiting access to educational resources, learning opportunities, and academic success.

In addition to economic status, academic performance also varies by gender. In reading, AI female students' proficiencies (34 percent) were substantially higher than AI male students' proficiencies (23 percent), but were the same as males in math (12 percent) and slightly lower in science (21 percent for females and 22 percent for males; NMPED 2018). While AI female students have an edge in reading, overall academic difficulties for both males and females have a negative impact on educational attainment. In addition, NMPED (2018) showed significant discrepancies in academic proficiencies between AI students with and without disabilities. Students with disabilities performed at lower rates of proficiencies in reading (11 percent vs. 32 percent), math (6 percent vs 13 percent), and science (9 percent vs 24 percent) than their typically developing AI peers. The outcome of educational performance for AI students with disabilities in New Mexico is very poor. This is alarming in light of the report that the percentage of students ages 3–21 receiving special education was highest for American Indian/Alaska Native students (18 percent) nationally in SY 2017–18 (Snyder, de Brey, and Dillow 2019). Special education, as the only alternative for AI students who are underachieving academically, is not a solution for the most vulnerable AI students who do not have a disability. When high numbers of AI students are not reaching academic proficiency, lack of educational success limits opportunities for graduation, future career pursuits, employment, and overall quality of life regardless of the student's gender, economic status, or disability.

Finally, the Partnership for Assessment of Readiness for College and Careers (PARCC) assessments in 2017–18, which also assess mastery of Common Core State Standards in math and English language arts for students in grades 3–11, showed that AI students performed lower than any other racial/ethnic subgroups (10 percent proficiency in math and 22 percent proficiency in reading). New Mexico's State Plan, as described in the TESR report, is to "increase the academic proficiency rate of the lowest-performing subgroup, AI students, to achieve an academic proficiency rate of 50 percent or more by 2022" (NMPED 2018, 16). This ambitious plan will require significant efforts to improve education for all AI students in New Mexico. However, challenges in AI student achievement and efforts to address them are not unique to New Mexico.

Student Achievement in Arizona

Like their peers in New Mexico, AI students in Arizona underperformed in comparison to other racial/ethnic groups. The Arizona Department of Education (2017) provided data on achievement for fiscal year 2016 for students in third grade through high school. The report refers to the 2015 National Indian Education Study (NIES) in differentiating "high density" and "low density" based on AI student enrollment proportions. In "high-density" schools, 25 percent or more of the student body is AI; and in "low-density" schools, less than 25 percent of the student body is AI. Findings by the Arizona Department of Education (2017) showed that students performed differently in high-density schools (116 schools, or 6 percent) compared to low-density schools (1,818 schools, or 94 percent). AI students made up 52 percent in high-density schools compared to 48 percent in low-density schools. The percentage of AI students with passing scores for English language arts in 2016 was lower at high-density schools (11 percent) than those at low-density schools (21 percent). For English language arts, AI students had the lowest percent proficient in both high- and low-density schools in comparison to other racial/ethnic groups. Similarly, the percentage of AI students achieving passing scores in math was lower in high-density schools (14 percent). AI students had the lowest percent proficient in low-density schools (23 percent), and the second lowest (14 percent) in high-density schools. AI students at low-density schools performed better in their educational achievement scores in English language arts and math. By comparing high- and low-density schools, educators have begun to explore factors that contribute to student success in high-performing schools.

Achievement in high- and low-performing schools. Under the direction of the National Center for Education Statistics (NCES) through the National Assessment of Educational Progress (NAEP), the NIES provides information to educators about the educational experiences of AI students. Rampey et al. (2019) summarized the results of the NIES 2015 study that describes the academic achievement and experiences of AI fourth and eighth graders. They reported that the NIES study addressed how American Indian/Alaskan Native (AI/AN) students perform academically and how they see themselves in terms of their Native languages, culture, and aspirations. They also examine factors associated with high performance.

In their study of elementary and secondary schools nationally, Rampey et al. (2019) had 8,500 fourth graders and 8,200 eighth graders complete the NIES survey. Fifty-nine percent of AI/AN fourth graders attended low-density public schools, 33 percent attended high-density public schools, and 8 percent attended Bureau of Indian Education (BIE) schools. Likewise, 57 percent of AI/AN eighth graders attended low-density public schools and 7 percent attended BIE schools. Native students performing at or above the seventy-fifth percentile were considered "higher performing," and those below the twenty-fifth percentile were considered "lower performing" in math and reading.

Rampey et al. (2019) examined factors that were associated with higher performance and reported that higher-performing students were likely to have (1) a school library, media center, and a resource center that contained materials about AI/AN people; (2) more than 25 books in their homes; and (3) a computer at home. In addition, higher-performing schools included fourth-grade students reading books of their own choosing daily, and students for whom reading was one of their favorite activities. Rampey et al. (2019) reported that between 25 and 30 percent of AI/AN students were very interested in reading about AI/AN cultures. They reported that about one-half of AI/AN students reported never being exposed to Native languages. Approximately 47 percent of fourth-grade students and 52 percent of eighth-grade students indicated they were "never" exposed to AI or AN languages. However, students in high-density public schools (larger proportions of AI/AN students) were likely to indicate being exposed to their Native languages. In addition, 16 percent of AI/AN eighth graders reported having a lot of cultural knowledge, about 40 percent reported "some" cultural knowledge, 31 percent reported "a little" cultural knowledge, and 13 percent indicated knowing "nothing" about their cultural history, traditions, or culture.

Analysis of their findings indicated that fourth graders who were exposed to Native languages "often" were more likely to express a high level of interest in reading about their Native cultures. Eighth graders who reported frequent ("often") exposure to their Native languages were more likely to express a higher level of cultural knowledge. Results support the need to consider educational environments that support AI/AN students, and students from economically disadvantaged homes with appropriate culturally and linguistically responsive teaching and practices to maximize educational achievement. Examining the educational performance of students with varying levels of English and Native language proficiencies is especially important for identifying appropriate educational supports.

Performance of English language learners. The *Bilingual Multicultural Education Annual Report for School Year 2011–2012*, provided by NMPED (2012), summarized academic achievement data for AI English language learners (ELLs) in grades 3–8 and grade 11 who participated in the state's Bilingual Multicultural Education Programs (BMEPs). Achievement results for students in all grades demonstrated decreases in reading proficiency, math proficiency, and science proficiency over a three-year period. NMPED (2012) attributed the decline to changes in assessment and reporting due to standards adjustments in 2011. The report indicated that 28.2 percent of AI students were proficient in math, 32.5 percent were proficient in reading, and 21.7 percent were proficient in science. There was a significant achievement gap between AI non-ELL students in BMEPs and AI ELL students not participating in BMEPs. This report highlights the importance of considering proficiency in English as a factor in student achievement. It also supports the need to support AI ELLs by having students access grade-level instruction and meaningful academic content through BMEP models and instruction (e.g., dual language immersion, maintenance, enrichment, heritage, and transitional; NMPED 2012).

In summary, AI students continue to struggle academically and perform poorly when compared to other racial/ethnic groups in reading, math, and science. AI students with disabilities and AI students who are economically disadvantaged score lower than their AI peers on standards-based assessments. The achievement gap for AI students across academic areas continues to persist nationally and in two states that have large populations of AI students, including Navajo students. Student achievement in high-performing schools offers insight into the need to support language and culture in the schools. Academic achievement challenges in AI schools for the lowest-performing subgroups are complex and long-standing, and researchers and educators have offered their unique views on why these educational challenges exist as they relate to culture and language.

Perspectives on the Achievement Gap

Researchers have explained the problems that contribute to school failure in AI education in different ways (Reyhner 1992). Some researchers, for example, have argued cultural and linguistic differences (Swisher and Deyhle 1992) and cultural and linguistic changes occurring in AI communities (House 2002; Reyhner 1992) are the root of poor academic achievement for AI students. Other educators contend that the ambivalence of AI students toward their culture when "assimilationist (Anglo-conformity)" models of education are used reinforces school failure (Cummins 1992). Researchers have also reported that "cultural loss" and "language shift to the nonstandard dialect of English" have had detrimental academic consequences, and that the major cause of school failure is due to "students' failure to develop literacy and other academic skills in English or the tribal tongue" (Crawford 2004, 269).

LANGUAGE SHIFT AND EDUCATION

There has been a trend toward the use of English, including nonstandard English (or Indian English) varieties by AI students and their families (Crawford 2004). Linguists have reported that more AI children are not learning their mother tongues (Crawford 2000, 2004; Fishman 1991; House 2002; Krauss 1996). Of the 154 AI languages spoken by AIs in the United States, twenty are still spoken by people of all ages and considered vital (Reyhner and Tennant 1995). English is predominantly spoken by the younger AI generation (Crawford 2004; Holm and Holm 1995). For some AI groups, the characteristics of the Native language have been transferred to spoken English, which Leap (1993) described as AI English. Linguists such as Crawford (2004, 267) reported that nonstandard dialect of English has "displaced the ancestral tongue among younger generations" and today's parents "tend to be dominant in a variety of AI English; thus, their children learn this dialect at home." To be functional in the community may then mean that the use of AI English must be retained, thereby reinforcing the use of AI English in homes and schools (Leap 1993).

The status of the Navajo language exemplifies the need to focus on English-speaking Navajo children. In 1970, Spolsky (1971) reported that 95 percent of Navajo six-year-olds spoke Navajo as well as or better than English and 5 percent were monolingual English speakers. In 1992, over half of the 682 preschoolers in Navajo Head Start centers were monolingual in English and less than half spoke Navajo (Platero 1992, cited in Holm and Holm 1995). In 1995, about half of the students entering Navajo Head Start were speakers of Navajo, but unfortunately many did not speak it well, and some lost their ability to speak their language over time (Holm and Holm 1995). Despite growing up in homes in which parents and grandparents spoke Navajo, some children acquired little or no Navajo and chose to respond in English as a result of the decline in the "relative prestige of Navajo" (Holm and Holm 1995, 163).

Recent data from NMPED support the trend toward children not learning the language. In their *Bilingual Multicultural Education Annual Report for School Year 2011–2012* (NMPED 2012), the department indicated that based on Navajo language reports submitted by two districts on 3,007 Navajo students, 45 percent were "Non-Navajo Proficient," 20 percent were "Limited Navajo Proficient," and 5 percent were "Fluent Navajo Proficient." In describing languages other than English in their New Mexico State Plan for the Every Student Succeeds Act, NMPED (2017, 54) reported that based on 2015–16 data, "Navajo is the second most common language with 6,010 speakers representing 3 percent of the total tested population." NMPED has initiated efforts to determine appropriate assessments for the purpose of language and culture.

There are many reasons for the decline of tribal languages. *A Report on Tribal Language Revitalization in Head Start and Early Head Start* by the National Center of Cultural and Linguistic Responsiveness (n.d., 4) indicated that "a significant factor has been a series of colonial and U.S. government policies and practices designed to suppress Native American people and their languages and cultures." Assimilation efforts by the U.S. government included intentional efforts to isolate children from their Native languages, culture, and traditions. Language revitalization programs advocate for strategies to support language teaching and developing models to encourage use of tribal language in early childhood and public education programs.

The shift from Navajo as an ancestral language to English (House 2002) and to the use of AI English (Crawford 2004; Leap 1993) have had significant educational implications (Leap 1993). Language use in the home and community is important for understanding the academic needs of Navajo students, for they "resemble those of English learners" (Crawford 2004, 267) in that they come to school with "little exposure to Standard English or to literate uses of English" (Crawford 2004, 267). According to Holm and Holm (1995), many Navajo children who do not speak Navajo well are also not proficient in English, and this presents a dilemma for their educational performance, including over-referral to special education to support language learning.

SPECIAL EDUCATION

In this section, we focus on the demographic profiles of students receiving special education services nationally and locally in the state of New Mexico. The types of disability services in special education and percentages of students receiving them provide information on high incidence disabilities, which may have negative implications for AI/AN students. We conclude this section by discussing issues related to overrepresentation of AI/AN students in special education.

The National Center for Educational Statistics (NCES; 2019) summarized the following information on children and youth with disabilities served under the Individuals with Disabilities Education Act (IDEA) in May 2019. In SY 2017–18, of the students ages 3–21 who received special education services under IDEA, 34 percent of all students had specific learning disabilities, 19 percent had speech or language impairments, and 14 percent had other health impairments. Students with autism, developmental delays, intellectual disabilities, and emotional disturbances each accounted for between 5 and 10 percent of students served under IDEA. Students with hearing impairments, visual impairments, traumatic brain injuries, orthopedic impairments, multiple disabilities, and deaf-blindness each accounted for 2 percent or less of those served under IDEA.

The NCES (2019) data also noted the percentage of students who received special education differed by race/ethnicity. Among students ages 6–21 in public schools in 2017–18, a higher percentage of male students (17 percent) than of female students (9 percent) received special education services under IDEA. The percentage served under IDEA who received services for autism was higher for male students (13 percent) than for female students (5 percent). Among students ages 14–21 served under IDEA who exited school in SY 2016–17, the percentage of exiting students who received an alternate certificate was lowest for AI/AN students (4 percent), and the percentage of exiting students who dropped out in 2016–17 was highest for AI/AN students (27 percent).

In New Mexico, the most current information about students in special education was available on the Public Education Department website with the heading "Summary of Child Count in School Year 2018–2019." The data showed a total of 53,996 students ages 3–21 received special education services under IDEA; 6,607 students were ages 3–5, and 47,389 students were ages 6–21. Students with language-based disorders such as specific learning disabilities (45 percent) and speech or language impairment (17 percent) were the highest categories. In addition, 9 percent had developmental delays. Other exceptionalities were lower in percentage. In the preschool age range, 45 percent had speech or language impairment and 40 percent had developmental delays. Speech-language impairment ranked highest for children receiving special education in preschool. When children turn nine years of age, they lose their developmental delay eligibility. Based on educational testing, these students may qualify as students with learning disabilities if they continue to struggle academically. This may be one reason that the exceptionality, specific learning disability, is the largest category for students in the 6–21 age range. The racial/ethnic makeup of students in special education for speech-language impairment and learning disabilities indicates that over 5,000 AI students receive these services in New Mexico.

The NMPED "Summary of Child Count in School Year 2018–2019" also reported that the percentage of students served under IDEA was highest for Hispanic students (62 percent), followed by white students (21 percent), AI students (10 percent), two or more races (2 percent each), Pacific Islander students (0.09 percent), and Asian students (0.4 percent). Among students ages 3–21 years old, a higher percentage of male students (64 percent) than of female students (35 percent) received special education services under IDEA in school year 2018–19. In addition, 21 percent of students with disabilities served under IDEA ages 3–21 had Limited English Proficiency (LEP) status and 78 percent had a non-LEP status. The convergence of AI students with disabilities (i.e., speech-language impairment or specific learning disability) with their ELL status is intriguing as it may offer insight into the role of language across these categories, yet there is no data at present.

In summary, the state data help us to understand that students with disabilities whose difficulties relate to language use are the highest in numbers in preschool and school-age special education. A fair number of these children are limited in their English proficiency. This calls for ensuring appropriate support for AI students who are ELLs as well as appropriately assessing students who are underperforming due to factors such as cultural and linguistic differences or socioeconomic status. Nationally, states have struggled with ensuring that AI/AN students are given appropriate educational support in general education as well as in special education to maximize educational success.

Disproportionate Representation in Special Education

Disproportionate representation includes over- and underrepresentation of particular groups of students (e.g., American Indians) in special education. Overrepresentation of minority students in special education is a long-standing issue (Artiles and Ortiz 2002), and this has been a concern in AI communities historically (Freeman and Fox 2005). The Bureau of Indian Affairs (2000) reported that more than 18 percent of AI students in bureau or tribal schools received special education. In 1997, more than 10 percent of AI children in public schools received special education (Pavel and Curtin 1997). There has been a significant effort under No Child Left Behind to ensure that children are appropriately referred for special education and related services, yet the percentage of AI children served under the IDEA increased from 10 percent in 1998 to 12 percent in 2003 (Freeman and Fox 2005).

Nationwide, AI/AN students continue to be the racial/ethnic group with the highest percentage of students served in special education, and the numbers served in special education continue to increase. In 2006, about 14 percent of AIs (including Alaska Natives) received special education services, compared to 8 percent of Caucasians, 11 percent of African Americans, 8 percent of Hispanics, and 5 percent of Asian/Pacific Islander students (Alliance for Excellent Education 2008). During the 2013–14 school year, AI/ANs were the most frequently served under IDEA at 17 percent, followed by African Americans (15 percent), Caucasians (13 percent), and Hispanics (12 percent; Snyder, de Brey, and Dillow 2018). In the 2017–18 school year, the percentage of students ages 3–21 served under IDEA was highest for AI/AN students (18 percent), followed by African American students (16 percent), Caucasian students and students of two or more races (14 percent each), Hispanic students (13 percent), Pacific Islander students (11 percent), and Asian students

(7 percent; McFarland et al. 2019). From 2006 to 2018, representation of AI/AN students in special education increased from 14 percent to 18 percent.

Review of special education data suggests AI/AN students receive special education services at high rates. American Indian children are at risk for being overrepresented in categories of speech-language impairment and learning disabilities. Over-identification in these categories may occur when evaluators rely on the use of test instruments to determine eligibility. Researchers (Bedore and Peña 2008; Caesar and Kohler, 2007; Henderson, Restrepo, and Aiken 2018) have argued that standardized assessments can lead to the overrepresentation of culturally and linguistically diverse (CLD) students in special education. When evaluators misidentify children without language disabilities and inappropriately provide special education, the potential for overrepresentation increases (Chamberlain 2005). Overrepresentation is not only problematic for Navajo students living on the Navajo Reservation, but also for Navajo children living off the reservation, in that it maintains stereotypes about specific groups' educational abilities. Factors that contribute to overrepresentation include living in poverty and cultural or linguistic differences that are likely to be outside the jurisdiction of education (Donovan and Cross 2002). The most criticized factor that contributes to overrepresentation among CLD children has been the use of inadequate assessment practices and procedures in identifying students for special education and an overreliance on norm-referenced assessments (Kim and Zabelina 2015).

Assessment Issues

Problems with special education assessment procedures have been a concern for AI students. For example, Cummins raised the issue with regard to classroom and psychological testing, which he believed had historically "disempowered or disabled minority students" in that "achievement and intelligence tests located the cause of students' educational difficulties within the students rather than the educational interactions they encountered" (1992, 10). While the response to intervention programming supports special education referrals to examine educational difficulties, the practice of assessing students and determining their eligibility for special education has not changed significantly over the last decade.

Selecting appropriate assessment procedures for speech-language evaluations has been problematic. A number of factors, including situational bias, format bias, value bias, and linguistic bias, have potential negative impact on assessment, thus leading to erroneous diagnosis of communication impairment (Taylor and Payne 1983; Vaughn-Cooke 1986). Test bias occurs when tests have been normed or developed for use with populations that differ culturally or linguistically from those with whom the procedure is being used (Goldstein 2000). For example, standardized or norm-referenced tools may contain test items that are not culturally or linguistically appropriate, thereby contributing to test bias (Goldstein 2000). Inadequate assessment instruments contribute to problems in appropriately assessing and identifying AI children who exhibit language-learning and other academic difficulties (Westby and Vining 2002). Assessment instruments primarily normed on Navajo students, particularly students exposed to their Native language and English, do not exist (Westby and Vining 2002). Therefore, because of the lack of appropriate instruments, students are evaluated using existing assessment batteries that are typically normed on monolingual speakers of English (Goldstein 2000; Roseberry-McKibben 1995). Using standardized instruments becomes problematic when they merely assess how well children from diverse backgrounds use standard American English (Goldstein 2000). Due to the problems inherent in standardized test instruments, it is often difficult to distinguish whether a student exhibits a language/learning disorder or whether poor academic performance is related to cultural or linguistic differences (Roseberry-McKibben 1995). The practice of administering inappropriate assessment measures and not taking into consideration cultural and linguistic differences in assessing language and literacy skills may ultimately contribute to misidentification (Westby and Vining 2002).

Language Assessment of Navajo Children

The Navajo Nation is one of the largest AI reservations in the United States, comprising 27,425 square miles (Navajo Epidemiology Center 2013). For SLPs who are not familiar with the Navajo language, identifying Navajo children with developmental language delays (DLDs) can sometimes be a daunting task. Evaluating Navajo children who may be English-only speakers, dual language learners of Navajo and English, or perhaps Navajo-only speakers presents a unique challenge. SLPs on the Navajo Reservation may have to rely on standardized assessment instruments that are normed on mainstream English-speaking children (Henderson, Restrepo, and Aiken 2018). Standardized assessments, deemed fair and unbiased, have become the most prevalent forms of assessments of academic performances (Kim and Zabelina 2015). As stated earlier, the danger of this practice is that AI children are at risk of being overrepresented in special education (Faircloth and Tippeconnic 2000; Finn 1982; Snyder, de Brey, and Dillow 2018; Yates 1988).

Identifying Language Difference from Developmental Language Delay

Speech-language pathologists need to recognize and distinguish between language difference and DLD so they may precisely classify Navajo children as typical developing (TD) or as having DLD. Paul, Norbury, and Gosse (2018) define language difference as a language that mirrors a principal governing language style that differs from the mainstream culture. Developmental language delay is defined as "impaired comprehension and/or use of a spoken, written, and/or other symbol system. The disorder may involve (1) the form of language (phonology, morphology, and syntax), (2) the content of language (semantics), and/or (3) the function of language in communication (pragmatics), in any combination" (American Speech-Language-Hearing Association 1993, 40). Discriminating language difference from developmental language delays requires an understanding of how Navajo children may perform on standardized language assessment measures.

Norm-Referenced Standardized Assessments

Typically, testers administer an assessment, score the assessment, and interpret the assessment with a specific method to validate the assessment results. To determine validation of an assessment, the norming group should be composed of the general population (Chamberlain 2005). Speech-language pathologists on the Navajo Reservation address language skills using many available assessments; however, these assessments may have items that reflect cultural and linguistic biases and therefore may negatively affect the Navajo child's performance on the assessment (Henderson, Restrepo, and Aiken 2018). Standardized language assessment with normative data for the Navajo population is nonexistent. This is unfortunate because normative data for the Navajo population could potentially decrease the overrepresentation in special education (Henderson, Restrepo, and Aiken 2018). Normative data do not exist even for Navajo children who are monolingual and monocultural English speakers.

Speech-language pathologists largely use standardized assessments to identify Navajo children as having DLD. According to Betz, Eickhoff, and Sullivan (2013), the most commonly used assessment tool among SLPs is the *Clinical Evaluation of Language Fundamentals—Fourth Edition* (CELF-4; Wiig, Secord, and Semel 2003) due to its psychometric characteristics—reliability, validity, and diagnostic accuracy. In addition, SLPs frequently use the *Peabody Picture Vocabulary Test, Fourth Edition* (PPVT-4; Dunn and Dunn 2007) as part of the assessment process, despite concerns of cultural bias (Betz, Eickhoff, and Sullivan 2013). However, researchers have not adequately addressed the validity of these assessments among Navajo students. Within the AI context, little research has investigated the appropriateness of using norm-referenced instruments with Navajo children. Currently, many assessment tools are normed with non-Indigenous, mainstream, English-speaking children and are inappropriate for Navajo children (Henderson and Restrepo 2016). Standardized assessments are attractive to SLPs because they can make comparisons of language abilities to determine if a child is significantly behind the students in the general population. However, current standardized language assessments are often poor indicators of Navajo children's true language abilities, since standardized assessments do not match their culture, language patterns, learning styles, and strengths (Henderson, Restrepo, and Aiken 2018).

Clinical Evaluation of Language Fundamentals–Fourth Edition. Henderson and Restrepo (2016) examined whether the CELF-4 accurately classified Navajo children with DLD and children with TD language when compared to the national norm. Thirty-one five- to eight-year-old reservation-residing Navajo children who had normal hearing and intellectual performance on the *Wechsler Nonverbal Scale of Ability* (Wechsler and Naglieri 2006) participated. Participants classified as TD versus having DLD based on a four-criterion diagnostic battery.

The standard score did not predict classification for all TD children; eighteen of the thirty-one TD Navajo children were identified as DLD when compared to the norm on the CELF-4. The three who were identified as TD had an average score of 85 (SS = 85, 85, 86). Their study indicated that Navajo children scored at or one point above the recommended cutoff score. Specifically, the average standard score of the CELF-4 for TD Navajo children was 76 percent (Henderson and Restrepo 2016). Further, their findings indicated that the mean of TD Navajo children fell 1 SD below the mean. Their findings are consistent with arguments that standardized assessments over-identify AI children as having DLD (Henderson and Restrepo 2016; Vining et al. 2017; Westby and Vining 2002). In contrast, all ten Navajo children with DLD were identified as having DLD when compared to the norm of the CELF-4. The average standard score on the CELF-4 for Navajo children with DLD was 50 percent, indicating that Navajo children with DLD fell 3 SD below the national norm (Henderson and Restrepo 2016).

The use of the recommended cutoff score of 85 for determining the need for a student receiving special education services resulted in the over-identification of TD Navajo children and classification accuracy was poor, which does not meet the recommendation by Plante and Vance (1994). Generally, Navajo children with DLD and TD language are not distinguishable from each other on the standard scores of the CELF-4 (Henderson and Restrepo 2016). Establishing a new cutoff score at 75 helped the evaluators to accurately classify 100 percent of TD Navajo children. While setting new cutoffs may be beneficial, the development of an assessment that is culturally and linguistically appropriate for Navajo children is recommended and preferred (Henderson and Restrepo 2016).

Impact of Navajo on the CELF-4. The Navajo language differs grammatically from English in several critical ways (Young and Morgan 1987). Even when Navajo children are not fluent speakers of Navajo, it can be expected that grammatical rules of their Native language are apparent in their subsequent English usage (Henderson and Restrepo 2016; King and Goodman 1990). This leads to specific predictions of grammatical differences among English speakers in a Navajo culture. Specifically, language errors on the CELF-4 indicated that Navajo children had difficulty with grammatical skills in the assessment, such as plurals, pronouns, comparatives, and vocabulary differences (Henderson and Restrepo 2016).

Navajo children with DLD and TD language had difficulty with pronouns. For example, on this CELF-4 test question—*The girl has a hamburger to eat. Tell me, who has a hamburger?*—participants commonly responded "The girl does" rather than "She does" (Henderson and Restrepo 2016). The children gave the precise gender when answering these questions, or they responded using the incorrect pronoun such as "He does" or "Him does." These errors might be attributed to linguistic differences. For example, in Navajo there are no gender pronouns (Henderson and Restrepo 2016). The general term *bí-* in Navajo simply translates to *she, he, it, they*; and *bi-/yi-* translates to *him, her, it,* and *them* (Young and Morgan 1987). Therefore, the English grammar (i.e., pronouns) may pose a challenge for a Navajo student who is learning Navajo as a second language or as a first language. Further, the Navajo language specifically addresses the person as "The girl is hungry" (at'eed dechiinizin), "Mary is hungry" (Mary dechiinizin), or "That girl is hungry" (Nilei at'eed dechiinizin + gesturing/pointing to the individual within context), which indicates who is being talked "about or to" specifically (Young and Morgan 1987). The single pronoun is not used in the same manner and frequency.

Navajo children with DLD and TD language demonstrated difficulty with plurality (Henderson and Restrepo 2016). Specifically, Navajo children struggled with irregular plurals such as *mice* and *children*; the children's exact responses were "mouses," "two mouses," "childrens," or "three kids" (Henderson and Restrepo 2016). Plurality in the Navajo language is not recognized by a bound morpheme or an irregular plural but is indicated by numbers/quantity (e.g., two mouse) (Young and Morgan 1987). Plurality modifies the verb in the Navajo language rather than the subject as in Standard American English. For example, "na'ats'ǫǫsí *nąąghą*" (the mouse is walking) versus "na'ats'ǫǫsí *nąąjááh*" (the mice are walking); *na'ats'ǫǫsí* (mouse) in the Navajo language remains the same in both sentences; however, the verb *walking* changes from singular, *nąąghą,* to plural, *nąąjááh* (Young and Morgan 1987). Language differences may explain why Navajo children had difficulty with plurals and misused singular nouns for plural (Henderson and Restrepo 2016).

Comparatives such as superlative suffixes were problematic for Navajo children with DLD and TD language (Henderson and Restrepo 2016). Children had difficulty with the following: *better* and *best.* For example, children were to complete the following sentence: *This picture is good, but this picture is even* _____, *and this picture is the very* _____. The participants' common responses were "gooder" and "goodest," which indicates that they had not yet learned the governing rule of comparatives (Henderson and Restrepo 2016). When comparing in the Navajo language, *good* translates to *yá'át'ééh* (it is okay; within that given context), *better* translates to *bilááhdi at'ee* (this is above), and *best* translates to *'agháadi at'ee* (this is above and beyond) (Young and Morgan 1987). Further, Navajo children with and without DLD had difficulty with temporal concepts such as *after, before, same time,* and *while,* which resulted in poor performances in following directions (Henderson and Restrepo 2016). For example, in the task that asks, *After you point to the shoe, point to the fish,* children first pointed to the fish, then the shoe, or only pointed to the fish. Culturally, oral directions are given in a precise and sequential manner, thus the example may be interpreted in Navajo as "'Áltsé aké bidinilchííd 'áko 'índa łóó' bididilchííl" (First, point to the shoe; until then point to the fish).

Alternative Assessments Among Navajo Children

Alternative assessments such as language sampling analysis and dynamic assessment should be used in place of inadequate standardized assessments (Henderson, Restrepo, and Aiken 2018). Conversely, these alternative assessments have no norms or validation with Navajo children. Recently, researchers such as Henderson, Restrepo, and Aiken (2018) began to evaluate the validity of a narrative dynamic assessment for Navajo preschool children. They found that although the measure yielded appropriate results (89 percent accuracy), the cut-score had to be adapted for Navajo preschool children.

Henderson, Restrepo, and Aiken (2018) investigated the classification accuracy of the Predictive Early Assessment of Reading and Language (PEARL) among preschool-age Navajo children. The PEARL is a dynamic assessment of narrative that examines language comprehension and production. In their study, ninety four- and five-year-olds were recruited and classified as having DLD or TD language. Henderson, Restrepo, and Aiken's (2018) study determined that the PEARL accurately classified Navajo children with and without DLD. Overall, modifiability and the posttest subtest story grammar were the best predictors in classifying between the groups.

Because there is no gold standard in classifying Navajo children with and without DLD, Henderson, Restrepo, and Aiken (2018) developed a five-measure battery classification system, which currently serves as the best classification for Navajo children. The five-measure battery included (1) parent report about their child's language ability at home and in their everyday environment, (2) teacher report about their student's language ability in the academic environment, (3) language sample that analyzed overall language (e.g., grammaticality, mean length of utterance, form, content, Navajo-influenced-English), (4) whether their participants had an Individual Education Plan for language only, and (5) the *Clinical Evaluation of Language Fundamentals Preschool: Second Edition* (CELFP-2; Wiig, Secord, and Semel 2004). Navajo children were identified as having DLD if they met four of the five-measure battery; and so, the CELFP-2 was not always used to classify this population (Henderson, Restrepo, and Aiken 2018). Further, TD participants were identified by meeting five out of the five-measure battery; however, they had to receive a standard score of 75 on the CELFP-2 (Henderson, Restrepo, and Aiken 2018). The CELFP-2's recommended standard score was derived from Henderson and Restrepo's (2016) study. Overall, the a priori classifications (DLD vs. TD) were significant (Henderson, Restrepo, and Aiken 2018).

Henderson, Restrepo, and Aiken's (2018) study confirmed that the PEARL discriminated Navajo children accurately with the modification of the pretest cutoff score, 10 to 7. However, the researchers recommended that the PEARL posttest score remain at 10. The PEARL pretest and posttest measured story grammar, language complexity, and episodes (Petersen and Spencer 2014). At pretest and posttest, the best predictor between Navajo children with and without DLD was story grammar. At pretest, Navajo children with and without did not receive episode scores; however, at posttest, both groups were able to receive a score for episodes. Episode results may be due to cultural differences in storytelling (Henderson, Restrepo, and Aiken 2018). Modifiability was the best discriminator between Navajo children with and without DLD. In fact, their study demonstrated *complete separation*; Navajo children with DLD received the modifiability score of 0, 1, and 2, and children without DLD received the modifiability score of 3 or 4. In sum, dynamic assessment best assessed Navajo children efficiently (Henderson, Restrepo, and Aiken 2018).

CONCLUSION

In the field of speech-language pathology, standardized assessments are commonly used to assess the language abilities of Navajo and other AI children in the United States. Language assessment of Navajo children using standardized assessments that are not normed on Navajo or AI/AN children continues. AI children are more likely to receive some type of special education service than any other racial group due to the administration of standardized assessments. Research by Henderson and Restrepo (2016) found that a commonly used standardized assessment among SLPs over-identified Navajo children as having a developmental language delay. Standardized assessments have over-identified Navajo children in speech-language pathology services, as they do not capture Navajo children's language abilities when compared to the sampling norm of the assessments (Henderson and Restrepo 2016). While tribes continue to struggle with appropriate language assessment, it is encouraging to know that alternative assessment practices may offer promising solutions. Henderson, Restrepo, and Aiken (2018) determined that dynamic assessment, an alternative assessment, was a viable procedure to identify Navajo children with and without developmental language delay. Research by Navajo investigators is leading to new ways of addressing educational and diagnostic challenges that have been problematic historically.

As Native SLPs, we advocate for improving appropriate assessment procedures among AI children. Improving practices requires expanding our knowledge base of cultural and linguistic influences on speech and language and speech and language development of typically developing Navajo and other AI children and developing clinical and educational practices that ensure appropriate identification of children for intervention. In addition, we recommend increasing the number of AI SLPs and researchers to address the gaps in services and research. Finally, we recommend improving collaborative efforts between AI communities and university programs to advance research, educational, and clinical interests that will have lasting positive benefits for AI speech communities.

REFERENCES CITED

Alliance for Excellent Education. 2008. *American Indian and Alaska Native Students and U.S. High Schools*. Washington, D.C.: Alliance for Excellent Education. https://all4ed.org/reports-factsheets/american-indian-and-alaska-native-students-and-u-s-high-schools-updated/.

Allison, S. R., and C. B. Vining. 1999. "Native American Culture and Language: Considerations in Service Delivery." In *Educating Children with Disabilities and Their Families: Blending U.S. and Mexican Perspectives*, edited by T. Fletcher and C. Bos, 193–206. Tempe, AZ: Bilingual Review/Press.

American Speech-Language-Hearing Association. 1993. "Definitions of Communication Disorders and Variations." *ASHA* 35 (S10): 40–41.

Artiles, A. J., and A. Ortiz. 2002. *English Language Learners with Special Needs: Identification, Placement, and Instruction*. Washington, D.C.: Center for Applied Linguistics.

Artiles, A. J., and S. C. Trent. 1994. "Overrepresentation of Minority Students in Special Education: A Continuing Debate." *Journal of Special Education* 27 (4): 410–37.

Arizona Department of Education. 2017. *Arizona 2017 Indian Education Annual Report*. https://www.azed.gov/sites/default/files/oie/files/2018/07/Arizona_2017_Indian_Education_Annual_Report_Rev_7-2-18_NG.pdf.

Bayles, K. A., and G. A. Harris. 1982. Evaluating Speech-Language Skills in Papago Indian Children. *Journal of American Indian Education* 21 (2): 11–20.

Bedore, L. M., and E. D. Peña. 2008. "Assessment of Bilingual Children for Identification of Language Impairment: Current Findings and Implications for Practice." *International Journal of Bilingual Education and Bilingualism* 11 (1): 1–29.

Betz, S. K., J. R. Eickhoff, and S. F. Sullivan. 2013. "Factors Influencing the Selection of Standardized Tests for the Diagnosis of Specific Language Impairment." *Language, Speech, and Hearing Services in Schools* 44:133–46.

Bureau of Indian Affairs. 2000. *Fingertip Facts 2000*. Washington, D.C.: Bureau of Indian Affairs, Office of Indian Education Programs. https://files.eric.ed.gov/fulltext/ED453013.pdf.

Caesar, L. G., and P. D. Kohler. 2007. "The State of School-Based Bilingual Assessment: Actual Practice Versus Recommended Guidelines." *Language, Speech, and Hearing Services in Schools* 38 (3): 190–200.

Chamberlain, S. P. 2005. "Recognizing and Responding to Cultural Differences in the Education of Culturally and Linguistically Diverse Learners." *Intervention in School and Clinic* 40 (4): 195–211.

Crawford, J. 2000. *At War with Diversity: US Language Policy in an Age of Anxiety.* Clevedon, UK: Multilingual Matters.

Crawford, J. 2004. *Educating English Learners: Language Diversity in the Classroom.* 5th ed. Los Angeles: Bilingual Educational Services.

Cummins, J. 1992. "The Empowerment of Indian Students." In *Teaching American Indian Students*, edited by J. Reyhner, 3–12. Norman: University of Oklahoma Press.

Donovan, M. S., and C. T. Cross. 2002. *Minority Students in Special and Gifted Education.* Washington, D.C.: National Academies Press.

Dunn, M., and L. M. Dunn. 2007. *Peabody Picture Vocabulary Test, Fourth Edition.* San Antonio, TX: Psychological Corporation.

Failing, A. M., K. K. Stice, and E. R. Inglebret. 1993. "Speech and Language Assessment Practices Used with Native Americans." Poster presentation at the American Speech-Language-Hearing Association Convention, Anaheim, CA.

Faircloth, S., and J. W. Tippeconnic III. 2000. "Issues in the Education of American Indian Alaska Native Students with Disabilities." ERIC Identifier: ED448009. Ericdigests.org, https://www.ericdigests.org/2001-3/alaska.htm.

Finn, J. D. 1982. "Patterns in Special Education Placement as Revealed by OCR Surveys." In *Placing Children in Special Education: A Strategy for Equity*, edited by K. A. Heller and S. Holtzman, 322–81. Washington, D.C.: National Academies Press.

Fishman, J. 1991. *Reversing Language Shift: Theoretical and Empirical Foundations of Assistance to Threatened Languages.* Clevedon, UK: Multilingual Matters.

Freeman, C., and M. Fox. 2005. *Status and Trends in the Education of American Indians and Alaska Natives* (NCES 2005-108). Washington, D.C.: National Center for Education Statistics, U.S. Department of Education. https://nces.ed.gov/pubs2005/2005108.pdf.

Goldstein, B. 2000. *Cultural and Linguistic Resource Guide for Speech-Language Pathologists.* San Diego, CA: Singular.

Henderson, D. E., and M. A. Restrepo. 2016. "Navajo Children's Performance on the CELF–4 and PPVT–4." Paper presented at the American Speech-Language-Hearing Association Convention, Philadelphia, PA.

Henderson, D. E., and M. A. Restrepo. 2017. "Culture and Language Consideration for Navajo Children on Standardized and Dynamic Assessments." Paper presented at the Arizona Speech-Language-Hearing Association Convention, Tucson, AZ.

Henderson, D. E., M. A. Restrepo, and L. S. Aiken. 2018. "Dynamic Assessment of Narratives Among Navajo Preschoolers." *Journal of Speech, Language, and Hearing Research* 61 (10): 2547–60. https://doi.org/10.1044/2018_JSLHR-L-17-0313.

Holm, A., and W. Holm. 1995. "Navajo Language Education: Retrospect and Prospects." In "Indigenous Language Education and Literacy," edited by T. L. McCarty and O. Zepeda. Special issue, *Bilingual Research Journal* 19 (1): 141–68.

House, D. 2002. *Language Shift Among the Navajos: Identity Politics and Cultural Continuity.* Tucson: University of Arizona Press.

Kim, K. H., and D. L. Zabelina. 2015. "Cultural Bias in Assessment: Can Creativity Assessment Help?" *International Journal of Critical Pedagogy* 6 (2): 129–47.

King, D. F., and K. S. Goodman. 1990. "Whole Language: Cherishing Learners and Their Language." *Language, Speech, and Hearing Services in Schools* 21:221–27.

Krauss, M. 1996. "Status of Native American Language Endangerment." In *Stabilizing Indigenous Language*, edited by G. Cantoni, 16–21. Flagstaff: Northern Arizona University.

Leap, W. L. 1993. *American Indian English*. Salt Lake City: University of Utah Press.

Long, E. E., and C. B. Vining. 2000. "Language Characteristics of Native American Children: Recommendations for Assessment." *Perspectives on Communication Disorders and Sciences in Culturally and Linguistically Diverse Populations* 6 (December): 6–10.

McFarland, J., B. Hussar, J. Zhang, X. Wang, K. Wang, S. Hein, M. Diliberti, et al. 2019. *The Condition of Education 2019* (NCES 2019-144). Washington, D.C.: National Center for Education Statistics, U.S. Department of Education. https://nces.ed .gov/pubsearch/pubsinfo.asp?pubid=2019144.

National Center of Cultural and Linguistic Responsiveness. n.d. *A Report on Tribal Language Revitalization in Head Start and Early Head Start*. Washington, D.C.: U.S. Department of Health and Human Services, Administration for Children and Families, Office of Head Start. https://eclkc.ohs.acf.hhs.gov/report/report-tribal -language-revitalization-head-start-early-head-start.

Navajo Epidemiology Center. 2013. *Navajo Population Profile 2010 U.S. Census*. Window Rock, AZ: Navajo Division of Health Navajo Epidemiology Center. http:// www.nec.navajo-nsn.gov/Portals/0/Reports/NN2010PopulationProfile.pdf.

New Mexico Public Education Department (NMPED). 2012. *Bilingual Multicultural Education Annual Report for School Year 2011–2012*. https://www.yumpu.com/en/ document/view/25212201/2011-2012-bilingual-multicultural-education-annual -report.

New Mexico Public Education Department (NMPED). 2018. *Tribal Education Status Report School Year 2017–2018*. https://webnew.ped.state.nm.us/wp-content/ uploads/2018/11/IED-2017-2018-TESR-Final.pdf.

New Mexico Voices for Children. 2019. *2019 NM Kids Count Data Book: Tending Our Garden*. https://www.nmvoices.org/wp-content/uploads/2020/01/NMKidsCount -DataBook2019-web.pdf.

Paul, R., C. Norbury, and C. Gosse. 2018. *Language Disorders from Infancy through Adolescence: Listening, Speaking, Reading, Writing, and Communicating*. 5th ed. St. Louis, MO: Elsevier.

Pavel, M., and T. Curtin. 1997. *Characteristics of American Indian and Alaska Native Education: Results from the 1990–91 and 1993–94 Schools and Staffing Surveys*. Research Triangle Park, NC: Research Triangle Institute.

Petersen, D. B., and T. D. Spencer. 2014. "Narrative Assessment and Intervention: A Clinical Tutorial on Extending Explicit Language Instruction and Progress Monitoring to All Students." *Perspectives on Communication Disorders and Sciences in Culturally and Linguistically Diverse (CLD) Populations* 21 (1): Article 5.

Plante, E., and R. Vance. 1994. "Selection of Preschool Language Tests: A Data-Based Approach." *Language, Speech, and Hearing Research* 36:15–24.

Rampey, B. D., S. C. Faircloth, R. P. Whorton, and J. Deaton. 2019. *National Indian Education Study 2015: A Closer Look (NCES 2019–048)*. Washington, D.C.: U.S. Department of Education, Institute of Education Sciences, National Center for Education Statistics.

Reyhner, J. 1992. "American Indian Cultures and School Success." *Journal of American Indian Education* 32 (1): 30–39.

Reyhner, J., and E. Tennant. 1995. "Maintaining and Renewing Native Languages." *Bilingual Research Journal* 19 (2): 279–304.

Roseberry-McKibben, C. 1995. "Strategies for Conducting Assessments." In *Multicultural Students with Special Language Needs: Practical Strategies for Assessment and Intervention*, by C. Roseberry-McKibben, 151–76. Oceanside, CA: Academic Communications Associates.

Snyder, T. D., C. de Brey, and S. A. Dillow. 2018. *Digest of Education Statistics 2016* (NCES 2017-094). Washington, D.C.: National Center for Education Statistics, Institute of Education Sciences, U.S. Department of Education. https://nces.ed .gov/pubs2017/2017094.pdf.

Snyder, T. D., C. de Brey, and S. A. Dillow. 2019. *Digest of Education Statistics 2018* (NCES 2020-009). 54th ed. Washington, D.C.: National Center for Education Statistics, Institute of Education Sciences, U.S. Department of Education. https:// nces.ed.gov/pubs2020/2020009.pdf.

Spolsky, B. 1971. *Navajo Language Maintenance II: Six-Year-Olds in 1970*. Navajo Reading Study Progress Report No. 13. Albuquerque: University of New Mexico.

Swisher, K., and D. Deyhle. 1992. "Adapting Instruction to Culture." In *Teaching American Indian Students*, edited by J. Reyhner, 81–95. Norman: University of Oklahoma Press.

Taylor, O. L., and K. T. Payne. 1983. "Culturally Valid Testing: A Proactive Approach." *Topics in Language Disorders* 3 (3): 8–20.

Vaughn-Cooke, F. B. 1986. "The Challenge of Assessing the Language of Nonmainstream Speakers." In *Treatment of Communication Disorders in Culturally and Linguistically Diverse Populations*, edited by O. L. Taylor, 23–48. Boston: College-Hill Press.

Vining, C. B. 1997. "Clinical Issues in Providing Speech-Language Services to Native American Children with Disabilities." *Perspectives on Communication Disorders and Sciences in Culturally and Linguistically Diverse Populations* 3 (3): 4–6.

Vining, C., E. Long, E. Inglebret, and M. Brendal. 2017. "Speech-Language Assessment Considerations for American Indian and Alaska Native Children Who Are Dual Language Learners." *Perspectives of the ASHA Special Interest Groups SIG 14: Cultural and Linguistic Diversity* 2 (14): 29–40.

Wechsler, D., and J. A. Naglieri. 2006. *Wechsler Nonverbal Scale of Ability (WNV)*. San Antonio, TX: Harcourt Assessment.

Westby, C., and C. B. Vining. 2002. "Living in Harmony." In *Communication Disorders in Multicultural Populations*, 3rd ed., edited by D. Battle, 135–178. Wolburn, MA: Butterworth-Heinemann.

Wiig, E. H., W. A. Secord, and E. Semel. 2003. *Clinical Evaluation of Language Fundamentals, Fourth Edition*. San Antonio, TX: Psychological Corporation/Harcourt Assessment Company.

Wiig, E. H., W. A. Secord, and E. Semel. 2004. *Clinical Evaluation of Language Fundamentals Preschool: Second Edition*. San Antonio, TX: Psychological Corporation/Harcourt Assessment Company.

Yates, J. 1988. "Demography as It Affects Special Education." In *Schools and the Culturally Diverse Exceptional Student: Promising Practices and Future Directions*, edited by A. Ortiz and B. Ramirez, 1–5. Reston, VA: ERIC/Council for Exceptional Children.

Young, R., and W. Morgan. 1987. *The Navajo Language: A Grammar and Colloquial Dictionary*. Rev. ed. Albuquerque: University of New Mexico.

CHAPTER 3

SAAD BAAHASTI

Our Language Is Holy

TRACIA KERI JOJOLA

THIS CHAPTER shares the journey taken by the To'Hajiilee community to revitalize their language and to use the process as a catalyst toward healing and creating a positive path for our future generations. To'Hajiilee (meaning "to lift water by rope and container"), federally recognized as the Canoncito Band of Navajos, is a small, rural satellite community located thirty miles west of Albuquerque, New Mexico. According to the 2010 Census data, the community is one of the 110 Navajo Chapters with a population of approximately 1,600 and a land base of 78,887 acres.

My professional journey began with To'Hajiilee (formerly known as Canoncito) in 1997 when I was employed at Canoncito Community School after graduating from the University of New Mexico. Returning to my community to give back to my Diné people was ingrained within my soul, and I was proud to be able to go home. My initial desire to become an educator stemmed from my upbringing, since my mother has been a teacher for over forty years. Having her as my role model positively influenced me to see education as a means toward creating long-lasting change within my community. In 2007, after spending ten years working in a variety of positions (education assistant, teacher, school counselor, and leadership team member) within K–12 classrooms, I chose to work toward my doctoral degree in educational administration. My dissertation, "Examining the Perceptions of Parental Involvement in Schools: Implications for Changing Roles of School Leaders from the Voices of the Community" (Jojola 2011), was an opportunity for me to work with my community and collect their recommendations and visions for their children's education. This study sought to gain more insight into the perceptions of parents and caregivers of Navajo children enrolled in either a K–12 tribally controlled, public charter, or Bureau of Indian Education (BIE)–operated school. The data gathered from the parent participants were analyzed utilizing descriptive statistics, and the open-ended responses were coded for themes. The statistical analysis identified recurring themes from parents and caregivers, which were that they wanted schools to incorporate more Diné language and culture into the school system and to provide more school activities that integrate the language. Parents' perceptions of language loss are also supported by language data received from *Ethnologue: Languages of the World* (Lewis 2009), which states that in 2000 the percentage of Navajo speakers was at 76 percent and in 2010 it had decreased to 51 percent. The potential imminent disappearance of our Diné language, at alarming rates, is disheartening and best summarized by Lilikala Kameyeleihiwa, a professor at University of Hawaii at Manoa:

> To lose your language is to lose the soul of your culture, and when the language is gone you are forever disconnected from the wisdom of ancestors; the loss of language inevitably results in losing the Gods you pray to, the land you live on, and your own government and sovereignty. (as quoted in Yaunches 2004, 1)

This quote by Kameyeleihiwa supports the overall desire of participating parents and caregivers who were advocating for more Diné language and culture to be infused within the school their children attended. Their statements demonstrated a collective concern that Diné language and culture were being lost, and they recommended that schools begin to include the Diné language throughout their children's day and within each grade level. To that end, in this chapter I describe two phases of a language project funded by a W. K. Kellogg Foundation grant.

PLANNING PHASE OF LANGUAGE PROJECT–YEAR ONE

In 2014, I returned to To'Hajiilee Community School (TCS) as the assistant principal after working with the Albuquerque Public Schools and the Los Lunas Schools. In 2016, I was selected as the principal/superintendent and the first local community member to serve in such a capacity. To'Hajiilee Community School, a tribally controlled grant school, is unique in that it serves preschool, K–12, and adult education students. Its average enrollment from 2014 to 2018 was 450 students from pre-K through twelfth grade, and 98 percent of the students qualified for free/reduced lunch; 98 percent of the population served were Diné students from the local community and the other 2 percent were urban Diné or Pueblo students from surrounding communities. This school is one of several that parents have available to choose from.

As I transitioned into my new administrative role, I completed the application for a language grant through the W. K. Kellogg Foundation, and it immediately became a labor of love. I could not believe that I was in a position to follow up with my dissertation and work toward the implementation of a language program within my own community. The emphasis of the grant application was to revitalize and strengthen Diné language and culture within our educational system and to structure it to include a systems change approach from the perspective of Tribal Critical Race Theory.

To provide some background for readers, systems change focuses on addressing the root causes of social problems and altering them to result in specific outcomes. As for Tribal Critical Race Theory, it focuses on decolonizing our ways of thinking, to redesign our educational spaces to highlight Indigenous culture, and to view our world through an Indigenous lens. These approaches were selected due to a desire to change and improve the quality of our educational system and to strengthen the self-identity of our Indigenous youth. Our areas of priority were to include the early childhood programs (which serve students ranging in age from birth to eight years old), our family engagement component, and our "grow from within" teacher training pipeline. We anticipated that we would facilitate from the perspective that a student's educational experiences influence the construction and formation of their Diné identity; therefore, through these Diné language and culture experiences, we intended to positively influence the construction and formation of a student's Diné identity, to stimulate positive attitudes about school and others, and to contribute toward improved academic performance.

Soon after submission, To'Hajiilee Community School received official notification from the W. K. Kellogg Foundation that we had been selected and awarded the $112,000 grant for our planning year. Upon notification, we immediately identified a team of highly capable educators with the necessary background to steer the project toward the goal of implementing the language program by the beginning of school year 2017–18. As a team, we then identified stages (or steps) to accomplish during the fall semester, venues in which to solicit stakeholder feedback, and potential immersion school sites to visit, and we anticipated outcomes for the project.

KELLOGG GRANT—Saad Baahasti'

Components:
- Language Revitalization
- Age 0–8 years old

Stages (Aug–Dec 2016):
1. Focus Groups
2. Surveys (Staff, Students, Community)
3. Individual Interviews
4. Establish a Language
5. Immersion Committee
6. Develop a Curriculum Team
7. (Pre-K, K)

School Visits Planned:
- Puente de Hozho
- STAR School
- Keres Learning Center
- Dream Diné

Venues for Sharing with Community:
- Chapter Meeting
- School Board Meeting
- Parent Advisory Committee Meeting
- Parent/Teacher Conferences
- Community Resource Meetings

Outcomes Anticipated:
- Revitalization Strategy Chosen
- Teacher Pipeline Established
- Student Dual-Language Cohort Recruited
- Early Childhood Language Nest Established

Next Steps:
- Pre/Post-evaluations completed
- Partner with Dual Language Educ of NM (DLeNM)
- Utilize Dr. Secatero's Well-Being Model

FIGURE 3.1. Steps needed for immersion program.

The outcomes that we identified would be the stepping stones toward solidifying a strong foundation for our program. Some of these outcomes included (1) identifying a language program design (language nest, two-way immersion, and partial or total immersion), (2) establishing a "Grow from Within" Diné language teacher cohort, (3) recruiting a dual language cohort of potential students, and (4) establishing an early childhood language nest within our preschool.

Throughout the beginning of our planning year we met biweekly to update the team regarding our progress and about any challenges we were facing. Our first challenge was identifying a survey instrument to utilize with our stakeholders. We needed one that was comprehensive of the feedback we were targeting (stakeholder support for the proposed school program, whether they had a child to enroll in the program, whether current students found the program important, stakeholder perception on whether Diné language is important, whether parents would be willing to learn along with their children, whether Diné language is important for their identity, identifying potential strategies for learning the language, etc.). Once we modified a survey instrument to collect stakeholder feedback, we began the process of seeking it out. Fortunately, we had a Navajo language consultant who had built positive rapport with stakeholders, so we had a good number of participants completing the surveys and participating in focus groups and individual interviews. It also helped that the consultant was fluent in the Diné language, that she was not originally from the community, and that she was motivated and vested in the project.

As we progressed through our planning year, we made it a priority to update our visual goal collage to help motivate us and to keep us focused on the implementation phase deadline. As the team collected stakeholder feedback, we simultaneously made arrangements to visit immersion school programs and meet with any programs that were supporters of language instruction. Our site visits to immersion schools were the most enlightening experiences of our planning year. Through the discussions with school leaders and instructors, it was more evident to us that this was an attainable task we had set before us. We gained more confidence as we moved forward and concluded, as a team, that there was no perfect time to start our program and that we just needed to choose to start and do our best. We also realized that our next challenge would be to create an immersion program curriculum.

In addition to the immersion school site visits, we made it a priority to attend second language learning opportunities, La Cosecha Dual Language Conference, Dual Language Education of New Mexico presentations, and bilingual education conferences to help our team maintain our knowledge on the recent research pertaining to language revitalization and instruction. We sought out any data on immersion school programs that could be shared with our stakeholders and school board members. In addition, we began to plan to apply to become a pilot school within the Dual Language Education of New Mexico network in order to continue to receive support as we implemented our program.

At this phase of our process, we decided that establishing this immersion concept within our preschool program would not come to fruition due to the limitations and boundaries set by our preschool funding source. It was disappointing, but through the advisement of the program director of our preschool, it was decided that the program would implement "Situational Diné Language Strategies" into the program to help support students as they transitioned into the kindergarten immersion program, if their parents selected it. Situational Diné Language Strategies is the practice of utilizing the Diné language during specific recurring situations that take place daily. These strategies were already being utilized within the Navajo Head Start programs around the Navajo Nation, and it was thought that this would be helpful and would provide the preschool program the extra time needed to seek other funding to support our goal of establishing a language nest. It was also during our discussion of whether total language immersion would fit our population that our team identified our elementary program as a perfect fit for a full immersion program. We all believed our school would serve as an ideal site since we were a pre-K through twelfth-grade program, since we already offered two classes at each grade level, and because it was supported by our school board and community leaders.

Now that we had completed most of our anticipated outcomes and had identified the grade level to begin with, we established a teacher cohort, completed school site visits, and continuously sought out professional development opportunities. Throughout these activities, we reminded one another to continue outreach efforts, to network, to positively support one another as a team, and to remain organized so that we would maintain focus. Once we felt that the survey, focus group, and individual interview phases were completed, we moved directly into recruiting Diné language instructors and interested teachers to assist with the development of a kindergarten immersion program curriculum. Our team decided to use our supplemental resource, Reading Wonders (a McGraw-Hill curriculum), as a guide toward developing a kindergarten curriculum that would allow us to track the curriculum standards as we moved forward. The cohort of teachers met twice a month to build the foundation for the Diné language immersion teacher to follow in the spring semester. As a team, we also decided that research supported the strategy that the first semester would be used to build language development and comprehension abilities within the classroom. The goal of the instructor would be to immerse students into the Diné language so they could begin to decipher the phonetics of the language and create a foundation of understanding. This was to be achieved by students being immersed in the Diné language daily and to also have the opportunity to watch the teacher and teacher aide model communication.

Although I do not have the data to share within this chapter, it was witnessed by all involved (teachers, teacher aides, administration, parents) that their children were learning Diné. Parents shared that their children were speaking at home, and it was truly an exciting period of time. As staff observed the classroom, they heard students communicating, and it was a beautiful sound. I want to stress that during the beginning phase of our program development, there was no widely used curriculum nor concrete instructions on "how" immersion would take place. We completed our research by meeting with various immersion instructors, programs, and individuals that we identified as "experts," and our overall interpretation of how best to begin the process was just to move forward. So, we moved forward.

As you can see, it was a fast-paced process for our team, and I will forever be indebted to all of them for their hard work and dedication to the initiative. It began as a labor of love for me and ended as one for the entire team. The development of the kindergarten immersion program was successful. We measured success by (1) having the support of stakeholders, (2) recruiting fifteen students to participate within our first cohort, (3) hiring a Diné language instructor with Diné knowledge and the skill set to teach the Diné language, and (4) drafting a curriculum that would be used and built on.

IMPLEMENTATION PHASE OF LANGUAGE PROJECT—YEAR TWO

We were very fortunate to begin our 2017–18 school year with a teacher for our immersion program. This was the most challenging component of this whole endeavor. We were afraid that our program goals would not come to fruition due to a limited number of applicants during the spring and most of the summer of 2017. I was beginning to panic since we had already recruited a class of fifteen students and had promised their parents that it would be a successful program. Fortunately, a Diné language teacher was identified, hired, and certified as a Navajo language instructor by the New Mexico Public Education Department. It was such a satisfying feeling to see the program open and our first group of beautiful students walk through the doors. We set up the program so that they would be immersed within the Diné language throughout their entire school day. They ate breakfast and lunch in a family-style setting, and a full-time education assistant was assigned to the classroom to support the teacher. A part-time classroom helper was also identified to support the students, and special classes (e.g., physical education, art, etc.) were designed so that their instructors would only speak Diné. It was not a perfect immersion situation since we had two teachers who did not speak Diné instructing them for thirty minutes each week, but it was a flaw in the program that we had to accept since we had no alternatives.

The first month was challenging for all involved. We had a parent who was requesting to transfer her child to the English-only class out of fear that her child was not learning to read and fear of low academic performance scores. Our immersion teacher was voicing concerns regarding the curriculum and the limited support available to ensure that the parents were reinforcing Diné instruction at home. We had a small number of supplemental resources available for the instructor and students due to the late selection of a teacher and overall limitation of Diné language resources (books, software, curriculum, etc.). For that reason, our teacher was working extra hard to create classroom materials and activities for student instruction.

As the year progressed, we did end up losing two students to the English-only classroom, but our program remained strong and many of our students were demonstrating growth in Diné language comprehension. We were receiving requests for program visits, and our parents were sharing positive feedback. The dream had been achieved, and we could honestly say that we had established an immersion program for the community. We soon realized that our work was far from done. We needed to begin phase three and start to produce Diné language instructors. The Diné language cohort continued, and our goal was to train a teacher to serve our first-grade students in school year 2018–19. We had four interested educators within the cohort take the Oral Diné Language Instructor Exam, and fortunately one passed.

It was turning out to be a successful year, and our future goals consisted of continuing with curriculum building, training more Diné language instructors, recruiting more students for each new cohort, and seeking out funding for future language immersion. Through it all, we continued to offer family engagement events focusing on culture. We involved our Parent Advisory Committee within the process to help educate interested parents in the program goals. We sent staff and parents to participate in professional development opportunities where they would learn about the benefits of immersion and be able to share that with other stakeholders. We never stopped nurturing the process, and it continued to be a success. We learned a lot throughout the years, and we still had not learned enough. We needed to learn more about assessments, curriculum, and how to increase parental involvement.

Today the program continues to grow, and this year the school should have implemented a fourth-grade immersion class and the fourth cohort of kindergarten students. Although I have moved on from serving as the principal/superintendent at To'Hajiilee Community School, I have not lost my desire to support language learning programs and the overall goal of ensuring the survival of our Indigenous languages. I am proud of the work our team completed during the 2016–18 school years, and I look forward to hearing about the future benefits of the immersion program for my community of To'Hajiilee.

Overall, Native language immersion programs need community input and investment in order to be successful. Such a program serves purposes beyond just revitalizing a language. These programs provide opportunities to instill healing and reverse assimilationist views that have stunted the self-esteem of generations of our Native people. These programs can bring community-based education back into our schools, they can reframe our children's thinking toward a Native American worldview, and they can strengthen our children's sense of place, increase resiliency, boost student retention rates, and improve academic performance. Immersion programs are bridges that can lead our Native communities toward a world where we can collectively work toward a common good and build more positive relationships that will foster future success for our children.

REFERENCES CITED

Jojola, T. K. 2011. "Examining the Perceptions of Parental Involvement in Schools: Implications for Changing Roles of School Leaders from the Voices of the Community." PhD diss., New Mexico State University, Las Cruces.

Lewis, M. Paul, ed. 2009. *Ethnologue: Languages of the World*. 16th ed. Dallas, Texas: SIL International. http://www.ethnologue.com/16.

Yaunches A. 2004. "Native Peoples Revitalize their Languages Using a Proven Approach from Across the Globe." *Rural Roots: News, Information, and Commentary from the Rural School and Community Trust* 5 (3): 1, 4–6.

CHAPTER 4

TEACHING THE HOME LANGUAGE

Establishing a Diné Cultural Identity

BERLINDA BEGAY

I N TODAY'S contemporary Navajo society, elements of historical experiences are still apparent, reflected in historic and present policies that are underlying influences that continue to shape sociocultural and educational issues. Brayboy (2005) constructed Tribal Critical Race Theory to address colonization through different contexts being prevalent to Native American education to meet student and teacher needs in today's contemporary world.

In order to be successful as both academics and as Native American people, we must maintain a strong sense of our identity. Our identity is rooted in our language, and the language carries the richness of Navajo culture and worldview, meaning Navajo philosophy. This holistic context is what is subtractive in Western education. Native American language education is unique because it involves methodologies that consist of our epistemologies, cultural protocols, and respectful practice. It is a unique type of culturally and linguistically responsive pedagogy that is not in the same category of today's Western bilingual multicultural education. Today's schools are dominated by Western ideologies that target specifically academic achievement, but Native American way of thought in education promotes and sustains lifelong learning to protect the cultural integrity and sovereignty of Native Americans. To include

Native American education with common bilingual multicultural education contradicts the objectives of survival and decolonization because it does not fit into Western common concepts and standards of bilingual multicultural education. We simply cannot continue the current practice of trying to fit square pegs into round holes because Native American education needs and methods involve a holistic view taught for the current purpose of survival of our cultural identity. Native American educational methodologies and pedagogy approaches have a different purpose involving decolonization that reinforces vital cultural values.

Language revitalization today means to restore direction to harmony with traditional, lifelong values to sustain life, because we must continue to remember that the devastating effects of colonization destroyed and undid the epistemological roots of Indigenous people. The loss of language is part of Native American identity in the twenty-first century. Native American language loss is increasing at alarming rates. Intergenerational transmission has become stagnant due to historic assimilation and acculturation efforts. The language shift today is a huge gap compared to fifty years ago. Today, our younger generation's first language is English. Although English is their first language, they fall into a unique group between English proficient and heritage language proficient. Today, they are primarily identified as English learners.

Today, whether or not Navajo students speak their heritage language, by benefit of their home environment and cultures, they bring to school rich sociolinguistic and intellectual resources that reflect multidimensional proficiencies and ways of knowing and learning. Students hear "Indian English" in the home and communities, and that is what they bring into their schools. Native American students are not well understood, respected, or recognized in the school setting. They are judged more strictly on the basis of deficiencies such as using Indian English in different facets of their core instruction and speaking related to English Language Development, which is the norm for Academic English that is utilized in standardized assessments. For this reason, they may be likely to be tracked into remedial programs or identified for special education programs (Begay, Adkins, and S. Nguyen-Wisneski 2019). Although Native Americans may not possess competency in their heritage language, they are likely to be exposed to it in a variety of ways through family and community.

In addition, many non-Navajo teachers who are teaching on the Navajo Nation know little to nothing of the language, culture, and abilities of the children. They struggle to find effective strategies for second language instruction and culturally and linguistically diverse instruction. According to research and practice, Native American students do better in school when their language and culture are affirmed and validated; this is what we call "culturally and linguistically relevant instruction" (Hollie 2012). Students whose home cultures are understood, valued, and respected do not feel marginalized, rejected, or isolated. Educating a student holistically is to address personal and cultural strengths that includes acknowledging an Indigenous student's historic experiences of their people and adaptation to social, economic, environmental, spiritual, and political change.

Eva B. Stokely, a K–5 elementary school in Shiprock, New Mexico, has the only Navajo dual language program in the Central Consolidated School District. Currently, there are 57 students in the K–5 dual language program. The program began as a magnet with a 90/10 dual language immersion model in 2011 with the goal of producing Navajo speakers and establishing a Diné cultural identity. The program started with a kindergarten cohort and added a grade each year. The program changed to a 50/50 dual language immersion one-way model when the fourth-grade class was added. In order to implement a state-funded dual language model, we had to plan for three hours of instruction in English and three hours in Navajo. In response to budget and staffing constraints, we met this requirement with three teachers instructing solely in Navajo and three who would be responsible for English language arts, math, and other content areas in English. Each day, one Navajo teacher taught three hours of Navajo to the kindergartners while the English teacher taught the first graders. Then the grades switched, so kindergartners received three hours of English and the first graders received three hours of Navajo. This model was the same for grades two through five.

FIGURE 4.1. 50/50 model for Navajo dual language immersion.

The Navajo dual language immersion program objectives are to support students as they develop a strong Navajo cultural identity and oral language proficiency. The program has chosen to put Navajo reading and writing aside and solely focus on Navajo oral language development to produce speakers of the language. Content area instruction is delivered in English.

The program now utilizes a unique curriculum based on the Navajo way of thought, developed by basing cultural instruction on seasons and moon phases. As an authentic reflection of the culture, only Navajo Nation Content Standards are utilized. Oral language development is based on the community's home language, the language that reflects the vocabulary and concepts of daily life with routines from the authentic settings of home and school. The program emphasizes a lot of play and language games to make second language acquisition and learning fun.

K-5 DUAL LANGUAGE CURRICULUM THEMES AND TIME LINE

QUARTER 1

August
- Classroom rules / procedures
- Colors / shapes and relative sizes

September
- Five senses / textures
- Four basic sub-clans, family / extended: kinship terms, relationships, protocols
- Sacred elements: fire, water, air, pollen

October
- Field trip: seed collecting, river, talk about environment, rocks, native plant uses

End of 1st Quarter

QUARTER 2

October
• Animals: birds, reptiles, fish

October–November
• Fall harvest
• Traditional foods / other foods
• Dress / jewelry / body parts

December
• Helping out at home and home environment
• Emergence stories

December–End of 2nd Quarter

QUARTER 3

January
• Coyote stories (morals) / cosmos / constellations
• Winter games: string games, *tsidił* (shoe game)

February
• Yikáí Yizhchí (Changing Woman) puberty ceremony (Kinaałdá): rules, responsibilities
• Twin warriors / Journey to the Sun, Kinaałdá ceremony: *táchééh* (sweat lodge), roles, responsibilities

March
• Clan history (creation of *bíla'ashdla'ii* [humankind])
• Home region/area: types of homes, cornfields, sacred areas

March–End of 3rd Quarter and Spring Break

QUARTER 4

March
- Continuation of home area /region / sacred areas
- Navajo history: Long Walk, treaties, assimilations, self-determination

April
- Navajo government

As the years went by, there were difficult times. Staffing was a challenge from the start, as the program needed teachers certified to teach both Navajo and content area instruction. We learned that when the same teacher taught both Navajo and English, students quickly realized they didn't need to make the effort to speak Navajo. For other teachers, multigrade classrooms and the need for extensive differentiation made it difficult to maintain Navajo language instruction as a priority. There was also much to learn about second language acquisition and methodologies for those teaching at that time.

Throughout uncertain times, as the administrators dealt with programmatic and administrative issues, the teachers stood in solidarity and worked together to build and strengthen the program. We found that teacher collaboration is extremely important for planning and materials development. Parents who believe in the program's philosophy are very active and supportive with program activities and initiatives. A majority of the students currently in the program began in kindergarten.

Currently a district bilingual and multicultural education coordinator, I was a former teacher in the program. I naïvely thought that as a fluent speaker of the language I could enter an immersion program and teach. I soon learned that it was important to know the foundation of the program's oral language methodologies and the theories, processes, and pace of second language acquisition. You cannot just speak Navajo— you must be trained in the foundation of the methodologies and theories. Since summer 2017, the language teachers have received intensive training that has resulted in a significant paradigm shift. Professional development and learning were led by consultants from the Indigenous

Language Institute and the University of New Mexico's American Indian Language Policy Research and Teacher Training Center. As teachers become more knowledgeable in oral language methodologies and second language acquisition, language learning becomes enjoyable, and students are motivated to learn their heritage language. For this reason, teachers must have a passion and love for their language in order to transmit that same attitude and approach when they are teaching. Through professional development, our teachers learned that one of the best ways to make language acquisition effective is to utilize hands-on experiences as part of an authentic learning process. This project-based learning encourages students to speak more. In order to provide strong language modeling, the teacher always stays in the heritage language and utilizes scaffolding strategies such as Total Physical Response and visual aids to communicate with the students.

Like all schools in the Central Consolidated School District, Eva B. Stokely has a heritage language model, but it also has the district's only dual language immersion model. In the heritage language model, students receive one hour of Navajo language daily. In the dual language immersion one-way model, students receive three hours of Navajo language instruction and three hours of content instruction in English daily. Some of the students in the dual language program are identified as English learners, and others are in the program voluntarily. While students in the heritage language model acquire some Navajo language, the likelihood of producing language speakers is small, because one hour daily only adds up to twenty-five days of total instruction in a school year. Those students who participate in the three-hour dual language model have a better opportunity to develop strong oral language skills, because three hours a day equals seventy-seven days of Navajo language instruction in the school year. Evaluations show that the dual language students are advanced in oral language comprehension and are able to hold a short conversation.

In both program models, it is apparent that cultural identity is also strengthened and evident in students' appreciation, respect, and honor of their Navajo identity. This positively impacts students' roles in school, in the family, and as members of the community. Parents are ecstatic and express their gratitude to the teachers and the school for the results they see in their children.

REFERENCES CITED

Begay, B., L. Adkins, and S. Nguyen-Wisneski. 2019. "Implementation Perspectives from New Mexico Districts." Panel presentation at "How Leaders Can Support Implementation of English Language Development," REL Southwest, Albuquerque, NM, October 29.

Brayboy, B. 2005. "Toward a Tribal Critical Race Theory." *Urban Review* 37 (5): 425–46.

Hollie, S. 2012. *Culturally and Linguistically Responsive Teaching and Learning: Classroom Practices for Student Success*. Huntington Beach, CA: Shell Education.

CHAPTER 5

EDUCATING FOR WELLNESS THROUGH THE PRACTICE OF K'É

TIFFANY S. LEE

I N A conversation I had recently with a friend, he shared with me a few incidents that concerned him. He and some of his peers travel together frequently out of New Mexico to attend various concerts of local rock bands. When they would meet other people from those states, he said his friends would often denigrate their home state of New Mexico, such as by calling it the crime capital of the nation or shame it for the level of poverty across the state. He said it angered him, and he said he now confronts them during those occasions in an effort to challenge their perspectives and change their interpretation. He said he loves New Mexico, his home, its landscape, its people, its cultures and traditions. We talked more about why he thought his peers would say these things to new acquaintances. He felt it had to do with their schooling experiences. His friends are Native American, like him, and Latino. They attended a large high school in Albuquerque with a predominantly upper-middle-class, white student population. He explained they were marginalized in that space and came away feeling shame for their community and state. Of course, this is his speculation, but this young man attended the Native American Community Academy, and he stated his views and perspectives of his home state were shaped by his school and family in important ways he felt his friends did not experience in their school.

I share this story to illustrate the impact schools can have on self-identity and connections to community. While this anecdote of the difference in perspectives between this young man and his friends does not implicate the entire public education system in New Mexico, the court case and rulings in *Yazzie/Martinez vs. the State of New Mexico* does (Evans 2019). In this case, New Mexican families sued the State of New Mexico for failing to provide an effective, sufficient, and equal education to, in particular, Native American students, English language learners, students with disabilities, and low-income students (Evans 2019). The families won the lawsuit. In effect, the state failed to comply with federal and state laws, such as the New Mexico Indian Education Act, and they were in violation of the state constitution by failing to provide programs and services to support students' success, such as culturally responsive education, dual language education, and important social services. Many scholars argue that public education in the United States, in general, has not been responsive to the needs and interests of Native American communities and students (Brayboy and Maaka 2015; Jojola et al. 2010; Paris and Alim 2017). It has dispossessed Native people of their lands in order to obtain tax-based revenue to build schools on Native land that support status quo curriculum and pedagogy that rejects meaningful integration of Native history and experiences (Bird, Lee, and Lopez 2013).

In this chapter, I aim to demonstrate the importance of creating educational systems that address not only the academic achievement of our Native American and specifically our Diné students but also systems that are more holistic and that are concerned with the overall wellness of our students and communities. We can integrate our Diné values and practices to ensure this holistic approach is culturally aligned and meaningful and that it counters oppressive systems. Diné scholar Kulago (2016) asserts that schools have a responsibility to engage with families and communities in ways that are in congruence with the community's collective practices. Family, community, and education are inseparable in this context when viewed through the Diné concept of K'é, a Diné family and community practice for showing love, care, support, and responsibility to one another (Kulago 2016). K'é is at the heart of Diné life, ceremony, family, and community. It is how we take care of one another through love, support, and sacrifice. My uncle told me a story exemplifying K'é from when he was a child in the late 1930s and early 1940s.

His mother, father, great-grandmother, and all the siblings would travel year-round to clan families around Crystal, New Mexico, to visit and take care of each other. They would stay with families for long periods and then move on to another family. This was a practice of K'é. Families supported one another and, in this way, created community. In this regard, relationships are a priority and reciprocal. Schools can promote student success by understanding, aligning, and actively engaging families and communities on principles grounded in K'é and a pedagogy of relationships.

We have models of former and present-day schools to learn from that value education for the whole child, or for shaping human beings who love their communities and who want to positively contribute to their communities. I will share what I am learning from one of these models in my work and as a parent. I have worked with and am a parent of children who attended the Native American Community Academy (NACA). This educational site has engaged in practices of K'é and relationships to strengthen students' ties to their heritage, their communities, and their homelands. I will share NACA's education for wellness approach with a specific focus on NACA's Diné language program. I then conclude with implications for Diné education.

THE NATIVE AMERICAN COMMUNITY ACADEMY

Located in Albuquerque, New Mexico (population approximately 600,000), NACA is a public charter school serving elementary, middle, and high school students. NACA opened in the fall of 2006 to approximately sixty students in sixth and seventh grades. It has served for the last ten years close to four hundred students. The majority of NACA students are Native American, many with mixed tribal heritage and mixed racial heritage. There are over sixty tribes represented by NACA students, and the one with the most representation is Diné. NACA students reside in all areas of Albuquerque, and many commute from local communities surrounding Albuquerque, such as Isleta and Sandia Pueblos and To'Hajiilee, a chapter of the Navajo Nation.

One important way NACA engages in the practice of K'é is through their mission. With the goals of serving the local Native community and

offering a unique approach to Indigenous education, the following statements on their website (https://www.nacaschool.org/) read, "NACA is
a small school that integrates culture, wellness, language, community,
family, and preparation for college into each child's education." This
holistic emphasis on the development of the child as a human being resonates with Diné ceremonial practices that evoke K'é. NACA's mission is
to provide a holistic education focused on "strengthening communities
by developing strong leaders who are academically prepared, secure in
their identity and healthy." Aligned with their mission, the school community identified six core values that are integrated into all aspects of
the school through the curriculum, pedagogy, assessment, policies, and
school climate. Those values include respect, responsibility, community/
service, culture, perseverance, and reflection. The six core values support
the overall focus on wellness for NACA students. NACA's articulation of
this focus reads, "Wellness is an important part of NACA's holistic and
integrated curriculum. It is implemented with meticulous attention to
provide the balance necessary for a child to truly succeed as a student—
and more importantly—as a human being." This emphasis on balance of
wellness in the schooling experience also resonates with Diné philosophies for achieving *hózhǫ́* (balance and harmony).

MY RELATIONSHIP WITH NACA

I became involved with NACA when I met with its founder, Kara Bobroff,
to discuss her plan to create a Native-centered charter school. She had
received an Echoing Green fellowship, which supported her as a social
entrepreneur and educator to lay the foundation for the school. Over the
course of her fellowship, she organized community meetings with families,
educators, researchers, tribal leaders, and other interested folks to discuss
the vision and mission for the school. Since that time back in 2005, I have
served on NACA's governance council, and I have worked with teachers
on curriculum and language education programming and planning. Most
importantly, I am a parent of two boys who graduated from the school and
an auntie to many young relatives attending the school now.

My boys both attended NACA since the sixth grade and graduated in
2016 and 2019. With the support of our family and communities, NACA

has influenced my boys to become more strongly connected to their multiple Native heritages of Diné, Lakota, and Cochiti Pueblo. While NACA was relatively new when they started and does not have the state-of-the-art facilities many other public schools are afforded, this did not deter them from loving their school because of the relationships they had with their friends, teachers, and the curriculum that challenged them to think critically and consider diverse points of view, all based on the foundational connections to Native people and communities.

I continuously connect my university students in Native American studies to internship and other volunteer opportunities at NACA. I have worked with NACA's language program in several ways. In 2008, I coordinated a summer language immersion program at the school for Diné and Lakota language learners. NACA was also included in the statewide study (Jojola et al. 2010) that I co-coordinated with a team of University of New Mexico and external researchers from 2008 to 2010 investigating promising educational practices for Native students as defined by students, teachers, parents, and community members. I have informally maintained interactions and discussions over the years in my role as a parent and governance council member with the Diné and Lakota language teachers at NACA.

The relationships I have developed over the last ten years with teachers, parents, and staff are not just as "researcher"; instead, they intersect my roles stated above in multiple ways. My primary purpose, along with other teachers, parents, and staff, is to support NACA and its students in building a community.

NACA teachers, parents, and staff engage in the practice of K'é by prioritizing the relationships they have with students, with one another, and with the local communities. In my research with NACA's language program, I found the program promotes K'é and relationships in three significant ways. The program promotes supportive relationships with each other (peer to peer, peer to teacher), understanding and upholding cultural values and protocols, and connections to land/place/communities. The outcomes of this relationship-based approach are the students' ability to connect their heritage language to each other, to the cultural values of their families and people, and to the land and community. The result is a transformative language education program built through their engagement of K'é, which aligns with the wellness philosophy of NACA. In the sections below, I elaborate on NACA's relational approach in each of the three manners specifically with their Diné language program.

RELATIONSHIPS WITH EACH OTHER

The Diné language teacher, Ms. Begay (a pseudonym to protect the privacy of the interviewee who was part of a research project), engages in the practice of K'é when she utilizes the students' friendships with one another to facilitate language learning. Through games and competition, they create a stronger bond with each other. Her method of introducing new vocabulary is to have students respond to statements they make about one another (interview with author, November 2, 2015, Albuquerque, New Mexico). For example, one student may state a condition about a fellow student in Diné: "John is skinny." John would respond, "Yes, I am skinny" or "No, I am not skinny." Other students can also respond, "Yes, he is skinny." It becomes a game and competition in that students are tested to be the first to respond and to show their correct oral use of the language. This simple activity that draws on humor and teasing strengthens the students' connections to each other and to the language. She continues this game outside of class, in between class periods and at lunch, with other conditions such as she or he is hungry, tired, tall, a leader, and so on. The activity is significant because it embodies qualities of K'é in which the relationship between students and the teacher becomes personal and family-like. The teasing and humor strengthen that relationship. Native people often utilize teasing and humor to teach the morals and values of the community and to celebrate life with one another (Deloria 1988). Ms. Begay's educational practice to involve teasing and humor reinforces the students' relationships with each other through traditional Native practices.

Beyond the language and general academic program, NACA reinforces students' relationships with each other and the school community through student clubs that are specific to strengthening students' youth and cultural identities. For example, the Hiyupo Alliance and the Sweet Nations are a boys' and girls' group, respectively, that provide activities for students to engage in self-reflection, learn skills (e.g., building fires, chopping wood, powwow dancing, singing, etc.), and develop their self-competency and confidence.

RELATIONSHIPS WITH CULTURAL VALUES AND PROTOCOLS

The Diné language program integrates Diné cultural protocols and values to reinforce language learning. They utilize "situational Navajo" (Holm, Silentman, and Wallace 2003), which is a form of role-playing using everyday situations and contexts for speaking the language. They also start class with a prayer or with a run to the east to integrate Diné-centered practices common in many daily activities and ceremonies. Through these activities, students develop a relationship with the language that is beyond simply learning the mechanics of language use.

Ms. Begay wanted her students to interact with elders to promote learning the language through natural, home-like contexts. This is an example of situational Navajo and K'é. She described one activity in which she had her students role-play and thereby learn the culturally appropriate way of interacting with visitors to their home. She said they learn

> the etiquette of when someone comes to visit you, how you tell them come in, *wóshdéé'*, and they shake your hands, and you also address them by who they are to you. If it's an aunt, uncle, grandma, grandpa, then you always ask them to have a seat and offer them a drink and something to eat. (interview with author, July 10, 2015, Albuquerque, New Mexico)

Addressing visitors through your relationship to them is a practice of K'é. This context helps students learn their Diné language through a culturally relevant and appropriate method that contributes to cultural continuity.

Interestingly, engaging students in some cultural activities to reinforce the language also presented challenges. Ms. Begay and Ms. Yazzie co-taught a summer Diné language immersion course and tried to integrate a number of culturally based activities. For example, they incorporated sand painting but found teaching the techniques and vision for creating a sand painting required advanced knowledge of the language. However, teaching through cooking or cleaning or other everyday household activities was more familiar for students and stimulated their connections to the language. Using the language based on how it is used by their family and relatives in their home communities gives the language a more familiar context, and as Ms. Begay said, "That way the kids can make that connection with the language and how language is used in a home, [with] livestock, just daily life" (interview with author, July 10 2015, Albuquerque, New Mexico).

NACA also reinforces students' connections of language to cultural practice through a biannual cultural exchange in Aotearoa (New Zealand). The eleventh and twelfth graders take this trip in the summer every other year, and during the school year prior, they have a required commitment to attend a special preparation class one to two times a week for an hour each of those days before the school day begins. In those classes, students are divided by their cultural heritage group (e.g., Diné, Pueblo, Lakota) and learn songs and dances specific to their group. The Diné group in school year 2018–19 learned to sing and dance a Diné basket dance and performed this for Maori relatives they visited with in June 2019. The preparation for their cultural exchange is another example of the practice of K'é in the programming at NACA. Students strengthened their sense of community and knowledge of their culture. It required their commitment, responsibility, and respectful sharing of knowledge and culture when they were in Aotearoa.

RELATIONSHIPS WITH THE LAND/PLACE/COMMUNITY

One complexity noted by NACA administrators is the urban setting of their school. This context provides more of a challenge for developing students' connections to homelands and the history, language, and cultural practices connected to homelands. The executive director stated they have to be very intentional in creating learning opportunities to develop students' relationship to land/place/community. Developing this relationship is a practice of K'é as it bolsters NACA's collective sense of community and NACA students' connection to the local region and land base, along with their connection to their ancestral homelands.

One example of this intentional practice is the school's yearly piñon-picking trip. Piñon picking is a common practice among Native peoples of the Southwest, and Ms. Begay shared how they integrated cultural protocols and Diné knowledge of the land during the event. She leads students in a Diné prayer before they begin and provides an offering of white corn to the trees and the earth from where they were going to take the piñons.

Ms. Begay said this field trip always excites the students, including those who were less academically engaged at school. Being outside, in the mountains, using the language, and connecting the experience to Diné knowledge involves students in a culturally sustaining educational practice that they enjoy. Ms. Begay indicated that many of the students had experience piñon picking with their families and were able to demonstrate their knowledge and fine motor skills and teach each other. The physical challenge, the cultural significance, the parent involvement (many parents chaperoned), and the setting in the mountains exemplified NACA's wellness philosophy in practice and promoted K'é.

IMPLICATIONS FOR DINÉ EDUCATION

The majority of Diné students attend public schools, whether they live on the Navajo Nation or not (Education Trust 2013). NACA is a public school that can provide some insights into how to implement an educational focus that prioritizes K'é, wellness, and an integration of Native values and cultural practice into the curriculum. Through NACA's practice of K'é, they reveal their love for their students and their aim to promote students' holistic development as human beings. While NACA understands their language program may not produce speakers with high levels of fluency (the language courses are one and a half hours a day), their objective is to develop conversational speakers who are highly motivated to continue learning their language. Their language program is transformative because it strengthens students' relationships with each other, with cultural practice and values, and with the land through their practice of K'é embedded in their wellness philosophy. They do this in a tribally diverse and urban context.

Their approach shows us that education for Diné students is best served when we draw on our own cultural practice and knowledge and integrate those practices and knowledge with the schooling experience.

Strengthening students' relationships through their heritage languages and practices of K'é provides additional resources for learning and for integrating Indigenous understandings of well-being. NACA is a contemporary example of self-determination in education expressed through decolonizing and culturally sustaining/revitalizing practices (Lee and McCarty 2017) and results in community-building for Indigenous peoples.

REFERENCES CITED

Bird, C. P., T. S. Lee, and N. Lopez. 2013. "Leadership and Accountability in American Indian Education: Voices from New Mexico." In "Leadership in Indigenous Education," edited by S. C. Faircloth and J. W. Tippeconnic III. Special issue, *American Journal of Education* 119 (4): 539–64.

Brayboy, B. M. J., and M. Maaka. 2015. "K–12 Achievement for Indigenous Students." *Journal of American Indian Education* 54 (1): 63–98.

Deloria, V., Jr. 1988. *Custer Died for Your Sins: An Indian Manifesto.* Norman: University of Oklahoma Press.

Education Trust. 2013. "The State of Education for Native Students." https://edtrust .org/wp-content/uploads/2013/10/NativeStudentBrief_0.pdf.

Evans, G. 2019. "Court Must Ensure NM Kids' Right to Sufficient Education." *Albuquerque Journal,* April 10. https://www.abqjournal.com/1301489/court-must -ensure-nm-kids-right-to-sufficient-education.html.

Holm, W., I. Silentman, and L. Wallace. 2003. "Situational Navajo: A School-Based, Verb-Centered Way of Teaching Navajo." In *Nurturing Native Languages,* edited by J. Reyner, O. V. Trujillo, R. L. Carrasco, and L. Lockard, 25–52. Flagstaff: Northern Arizona University.

Jojola, T., T. S. Lee, A. Alcantara, M. Belgarde, C. Bird, N. Lopez, and B. Singer. 2010. *Indian Education in New Mexico, 2025.* Santa Fe, NM: Public Education Department, Indian Education Division.

Kulago, H. 2016. "Activating Indigenous Knowledge to Create Supportive Educational Environments by Rethinking Family, Community, and School Partnerships." *Journal of Family Diversity in Education* 2 (1): 1–20.

Lee, T. S., and T. L. McCarty. 2017. "Upholding Indigenous Education Sovereignty through Critical Culturally Sustaining/Revitalizing Pedagogy." In *Culturally Sustaining Pedagogies: Teaching and Learning for Justice in a Changing World,* edited by D. Paris and H. S. Alim, 61–82. New York: Teachers College Press.

Paris, D., and H. S. Alim, eds. 2017. *Culturally Sustaining Pedagogies: Teaching and Learning for Justice in a Changing World.* New York: Teachers College Press.

CHAPTER 6

K'É BEE 'AHIŁ NA'ANISH

Mentorship While Utilizing a Diné-Centered,
Community-Based Participatory Research Approach

LORENDA BELONE AND VINCENT WERITO

THIS CHAPTER describes the experiences of two Navajo (Diné) researchers, one as an academic mentor and the other as a mentee and a new principal investigator (PI) of a one-year research pilot study funded by the National Institutes of Health focused on behavioral health disparities in partnership with three Navajo communities. Both researchers are tenured in their university, and the importance of sharing their unique experience is based on the fact that there are numerous barriers to scientific success that minority (e.g., Indigenous) researchers face when conducting health research (Shavers et al. 2005; Walters and Simoni 2009). One recommendation to overcome these barriers for junior researchers is mentorship, particularly by a senior researcher who is knowledgeable in navigating the challenges of conducting research in the academy and in tribal communities (Belone 2010; Tuhiwai-Smith 2005; Walters and Simoni 2009). This chapter provides background information on the research funding opportunity that supported a Diné-centered, community-based participatory research study and insights on how this research approach inspired the mentorship process that brought two Navajo researchers together. We also offer examples of mentoring experiences in the academy and in the field and discuss implications of mentorship in research grounded in a Diné-centered paradigm. The underpinning of the chapter title is "K'é Bee 'Ahił Na'anish," (translated loosely as "working together with the principles of K'é"), which involved a mentorship approach that was truly collaborative, reciprocal, bidirectional in the sharing of knowledge, and grounded in K'é.

BACKGROUND

The University of New Mexico's (UNM) Transdisciplinary Research, Equity and Engagement (TREE) Center for Advancing Behavioral Health is funded by the National Institute on Minority Health and Health Disparities for a five-year period (2017–22) and is one of twelve national research centers of excellence. The TREE Center is located within the College of Population Health and consists of three interdisciplinary teams: an administrative core, a community engagement and dissemination core (CEDC), and an investigator development core (IDC). An important aim of the TREE Center has been to support underrepresented minority junior faculty who are early stage investigators who have an interest in conducting transdisciplinary, multilevel intervention research that addresses behavioral health disparities with socioeconomically disadvantaged and underserved rural populations within the state through one-year pilot research projects (https://hsc.unm.edu/population -health/research/tree-center/). Each grant year, the TREE Center posts a request for proposals (RFP), funding the top three applications.

The role of the CEDC has been to disseminate the pilot project research findings throughout the state and elicit research topics of interest that are added to the annual TREE RFPs. Therefore, an important role of the CEDC has been to "cultivate bi-directional learning and mentoring opportunities for academic, community, and tribal stakeholders aimed at creating intersections of community knowledge and practice with evidence-based knowledge" (https://hsc.unm.edu/population-health/ research/tree-center/about.html#cedc). The codirector of the CEDC is Lorenda Belone and in her role she has been actively engaged with two Navajo grassroots organizations, the Tri-Chapter Alliance and the Diné-Centered Research and Evaluation (DCRE) working group. These two organizations raised concerns about fracking activities in close proximity to several Navajo communities in northwestern New Mexico. Their work centered on shedding light on the potential behavioral, mental, physical, and spiritual health of Navajo community members in these areas that were being heavily impacted. In being responsive to the community and to the lack of evidence of adverse health effects due to fracking, Belone recommended to the working group the submission of an application for a TREE pilot study that required an early stage investigator from the university. Fortunately, Belone knew of a colleague in the College of Education and Human Sciences who was invited to a meeting in November 2017. In that meeting, Vincent Werito, who is faculty in the Department of Language, Literacy, and Sociocultural Studies, attended and generously agreed to lead and submit a behavioral and mental health intervention pilot study even though he had never written or submitted a health research study proposal.

Werito has many years of teaching experience with Indigenous youth, and his research interests have centered on Navajo education and language revitalization; however, lacking health research experience did not deter Werito. He was willing to invest his time and to learn about health research processes because he is from one of the communities impacted by the fracking. What resulted, after numerous revisions of the proposal, was a community-based participatory research (CBPR) study entitled "Developing Community Partnerships Through Research to Define Community Well-Being from a Diné-Centered Perspective with Three Navajo Communities in New Mexico," which was favorably reviewed and funded with a robust research team. While the RFP only required that the application include an academic and community mentor, Werito expanded his research team that included himself as the PI, Belone as his academic mentor, David Begay and David Tsosie (DCRE members) who served as cultural advisors/mentors, Daniel Tso and Samuel Sage who served as community mentors, and Mario Atencio as a community mentee, all in collaborative partnership with three Navajo communities. This chapter will share the mentorship experience of the study PI and his academic mentor.

TREE CENTER PILOT STUDY

The goal of Werito's pilot study was to create a community-university research partnership in an Indigenous (specifically, Diné) context by establishing a multidimensional, Diné-centered research infrastructure and framework through the utilization of a Diné-centered CBPR approach to explore well-being as understood by the community. In many Navajo communities, the collective tribal knowledge of the local community is often largely undocumented or underutilized in addressing educational and health disparities that in turn affect community well-being. Thus, this research study developed a process of engaging Navajo community members using K'é to engage in critical dialogue and praxis to address long-standing health disparities and explore community members' perspectives of well-being. An important aspect of CBPR is the creation of a local community advisory board to guide the research process and to have active participation grounded in local knowledge (Belone et al. 2017; Belone, Tosa, et al. 2016; Wallerstein and Duran 2006; Werito and Belone 2021). Upon funding of the study, members from the three Navajo communities were invited to participate on a community advisory research team (CART).

Key findings of the study were the knowledge gained about community-engaged research from a Diné perspective, a local definition of community well-being, and the significance of "elder" knowledge for the recovery of traditional ecological knowledge to address education and health disparities. As the Diné (Navajo) Nation begins to take control of their schools and health services moving toward local governance, Diné communities must engage in research and plan ahead for themselves while utilizing local community knowledge for sustainability.

COMMUNITY-BASED PARTICIPATORY RESEARCH FROM A DINÉ PERSPECTIVE

Research with American Indian/Alaska Native (AI/AN) communities has increasingly turned to CBPR approaches to reduce health disparities and strengthen community wellness (Belone et al. 2017; Belone, Tosa, et al. 2016; Blue Bird Jernigan et al. 2015; Hicks et al. 2012; Wallterstein, Oetzel, et al. 2019; Walters and Simoni 2009; Walters et al. 2018). A central tenet of CBPR is that it is not a specific research method but an orientation, a research process paradigm that challenges the roles of the researcher and those being researched by examining the traditional roles of power and participation, who is included or excluded, and who is developing and leading the research agenda, and as such, hopefully reducing mistrust between the academy and the community (Lucero et al. 2018; Wallerstein, Muhammad, et al. 2019; Wallerstein, Oetzel, et al. 2019). According to Israel et al. (2013), the key principles of CBPR are that it (1) recognizes community as a unit of identity; (2) builds on strengths and resources within the community; (3) facilitates collaborative, equitable partnership in all research phases and involves an empowering and power-sharing process that attends to social inequalities; (4) promotes co-learning and capacity building among all partners; (5) integrates and achieves a balance between research and action for the mutual benefit of all partners; (6) emphasizes public health problems of local relevance and ecological perspectives that attend to the multiple determinants of health and disease; (7) involves systems development through a cyclical and iterative process; (8) disseminates findings and knowledge gained to all partners and involves all partners in the dissemination process; (9) requires a long-term process and commitment to sustainability; and (10) addresses issues of race, ethnicity, racism, and social class and embraces "cultural humility."

The DCRE approach resonates with CBPR in that the Diné-centered understanding of seeking knowledge for life's sake, and as research, reaffirms the Diné community cultural core values of honoring relationships, practicing reciprocity, developing critical inquiry, and always striving for harmonious outcomes (Emerson 2014; Werito 2014; Werito and Belone 2021). For example, in reference to the purpose of conducting research, the late Larry Emerson shared with the PI during his dissertation study how the goal of Indigenous research should always be to achieve harmonious outcomes. That is, when engaging in a search for knowledge, a Diné paradigm emphasizes a search of coming to and going back to *hózhǫ́*, or a state or place of balance and peace. Further, when this approach is embedded within a framework of K'é (Kahn-John and Koithan 2015), the lifelong process of searching for knowledge that is critical, intuitive, reflexive, and reaffirming will inherently benefit the larger community of relationships. Kahn-John and Koithan (2015, 25) describe K'é as the "honoring of relationships . . . requiring a constant awareness of the relationships and interconnectedness between one and the environment (others, family, community, tribe, spirits, people of the world, all living creatures, nature, and the universe)."

MENTORSHIP: WALKING THE CBPR TALK

NAVIGATING RESEARCH IN THE ACADEMY
Proposal Writing

It is important to mention that Werito and Belone had established their clan relationship as nephew and aunt through a shared clan group soon after they met. So, when Belone recommended and encouraged Werito to take on the role of PI of the pilot study, he agreed based on his respect for her expertise and knowledge and trust of her guidance. Mentorship occurred immediately upon Werito's decision to take on the PI role, first in the writing of the proposal that needed to be written in a National Institutes of Health (NIH) format. Fortunately, Belone had experience writing and obtaining NIH-funded research grants and is considered a mid-career researcher who has two R01 research studies (2014–21 and 2020–25) with several tribal communities and has utilized a CBPR approach with an Indigenous paradigm for the past twenty-one years in health disparities research. Moreover, her experiences with community engagement have been largely informed by her own growing understanding of K'é, especially in how she relates to others in these communities. CBPR recommends collaboration in all phases of the research process including the writing of the research proposal, which Werito adhered to through meetings with the research team (cultural advisors, community mentors, and mentee) in the drafting of the proposal. Werito also presented the proposal to the local governing bodies (i.e., chapter houses) to gain approval through chapter resolutions that were added to the proposal for submission.

Institutional Review Boards

Upon receiving approval for funding from the TREE Center, Werito was required to obtain approval from two institutional review boards (IRB): UNM and the Navajo Nation's Human Research Review Board (HRRB). Werito soon learned how to write a health-focused research protocol with Belone's assistance and mentorship, and he was familiar with the UNM submission, review, and approval process, which was completed electronically. However, he was unfamiliar with the Navajo Nation's process that required one original and ten copies of the application cover, an abstract, and six descriptive sections: community involvement, benefits to the Navajo Nation, research project description, informed consent form(s), certification of the PI, and study attachments that included curriculum vitae(s), resolutions, approved academic IRB letter, and a budget (Becenti-Pigman et al. 2008). Werito had not experienced submitting a Navajo application, which required either hand carrying or mailing the hard copies for placement on their monthly agenda and an in-person presentation so that travel from Albuquerque to Window Rock, Arizona, was needed. Therefore, Belone accompanied Werito and prepped him in what to expect since she had an active Navajo research study. On the day of the meeting Werito was able to share with the board the purpose of his study in both English and Navajo, and the board gave their approval with no recommended changes, which does not occur often. As they left the meeting, Werito told Belone, "Thank you for letting me hang onto your coat tails," to which she jokingly responded that it was not her coat tails but her Navajo skirt, three tiered and calico, so that together they found a new use for the skirt besides the traditional use of wiping grandchildren's tears or running noses, which made them both laugh—and laughter and teasing are grounded in K'é. To celebrate obtaining approval, the pair enjoyed a bowl of mutton stew and frybread at a local food vendor's stand. During their meal, Belone shared that she was impressed with how the madam chair, Ms. Pigman, responded so positively to his presentation, which was mostly in Navajo and required deep knowledge about research from both Western and Diné perspectives. Belone was also impressed with how Werito was able to fully answer all the questions posed by the board and how he was able to present himself as a capable Navajo scholar/researcher.

NAVIGATING RESEARCH IN THE FIELD

CBPR Research Process

Annually, Belone co-teaches a UNM graduate-level CBPR summer institute in which Werito had participated in the past. Upon receiving funding for his pilot study, this provided a great opportunity to put into practice what he had learned. The study included the following CBPR activities: (1) recruitment of community members to create an active CART to guide the research process, (2) assessment of community research capacity and engagement by administering the CBPR community engagement survey, (3) bidirectional teachings by and with the CART members, (4) a culturally centered approach in the development of a well-being model,

(5) sharing of research findings in community forums, and (6) dissemination of research findings at research conferences with available research team members (mentors and mentee).

In utilizing a CBPR approach, the study quickly established a CART with members from the three Navajo communities (including young adults, parents, and elders), service providers who worked in the communities (e.g., health, social service, education), and key stakeholders (e.g., Navajo members of grassroots organizations working in the community). During the recruitment process, Werito would often ask if it was going correctly and Belone would assure him that each community was different and that the team would organically come together based on the participants' level of interest. Werito was also continually concerned about the size of the CART, but Belone assured him that it was not the size but the participants that mattered. In the end, a vibrant CART was established and was able to assist Werito in navigating the research process, ensuring a culturally responsive research agenda and design. Although not all of the CART members were present at every meeting, the group did have continued participation by key community members who had an active voice in data collection, analyses, and dissemination. Belone and Werito traveling out to the communities for CART meetings allowed for a great opportunity to discuss challenges and plans for the next steps in the research process. When traveling back from the communities, the discussion focused on their experiences of the meeting and any interpretation or explanation of any unclear comments in addition to the practicing of reflexivity, focusing on their role as researchers and their position of power and privilege, an often-used practice by CBPR practitioners (Belone, Lucero, et al. 2016; Chandanabhumma et al. 2020; Wallerstein, Oetzel, et al. 2019).

IMPLICATIONS

ADVANCING A DINÉ-CENTERED, COMMUNITY-ENGAGED RESEARCH DESIGN THROUGH MENTORSHIP

Learning and applying the principles of CBPR can be an arduous task for any researcher, especially an early stage researcher. However, Werito found the experience to be pragmatic, from writing the research proposal to the completion of the study that he believed to only be possible due to the guidance and support from his mentor who had the skills and knowledge in navigating research both within the academy and with tribal communities, but more importantly a mentor who was Diné and related by clan and one who could be approached as an aunt whenever advice was sought. The lessons learned by the mentor and mentee were bidirectional in that as a CBPR researcher, Belone was eager to learn about what worked and what the challenges were for Werito as he navigated the research process with his own community and the neighboring communities for mutual benefit and harmonious outcomes. Further, both researchers learned that K'é can be used within an academic research context.

Having a Diné mentor who was also a CBPR researcher aided in the process of writing a proposal from a Diné-centered perspective by being able to highlight the following: who is the community, what partnerships existed and which need to be developed, and why it is important to share with the community the mutual benefits for participating in the research study? The Navajo Nation's HRRB research policies echo the CBPR principles of building a partnership with the community, ensuring mutual benefit for all involved in the research project, focusing on health issues that are of importance to the community, and sharing the research findings and knowledge gained by the research partners. Thus, knowledge production as in research from a Diné paradigm ensures that knowledge or ways of knowing do not belong to one individual and should be shared with all. Moreover, this approach is central to the tenets of K'é that honor relationships, responsibility, and trustworthiness (being a kind and helpful relative to others).

The mentorship was informed by the research process and the overarching goal of hózhǫ́ and creating balance and harmony, which was often reiterated by all members of the research team. For example, it was essential to the CART and the research team of mentors and mentee that the process be informed by Diné principles of K'é so that data collection and analysis were conducted respectfully based on clan relationships, the caveat being that talking to community members and asking questions about their lives to find answers or possibly more questions or resolutions should not be conducted in a way that was impersonal but instead used K'é. Therefore, the focus group interviews with community members were conducted by using a "talking circle" format where everyone was given an opportunity to talk and share their voice in a manner that was guided by cultural protocols of respect. Furthermore, the interview questions were translated from English to Navajo primarily for the benefit of elders who did not always feel comfortable speaking English.

The mentorship relationship did not end when the study ended; instead, it continues to grow as Werito expands his research experience. In the past year he was awarded funds from UNM for a study that was informed by the CART that focuses on "successful aging" and how Navajo elders from his community understand and reflect this concept. Werito continues to disseminate the findings from his pilot study and co-writes manuscripts (Werito and Belone 2021) and book chapters with his mentor. Werito also continues to work with the three Navajo communities and plans to co-develop a community profile assessment, hoping that the findings can inform future CBPR research studies that are focused on education, economics, governance, and health. Belone recently received funding from the National Institute on Minority Health and Health Disparities (2020–25) for a five-year research study to examine the dissemination and implementation of an evidence-based Indigenous family program in which the child participants (fourth and fifth graders) have reported an enhanced connection to school and family through strengthened culture and language connectedness and active participation in family projects that benefit their communities (Belone et al. 2020). Werito currently serves as a co-investigator on this important study with six Southwest tribal communities.

ACKNOWLEDGMENTS

We deeply appreciate our community advisory research team, the two community mentors (Daniel Tso and Sam Sage), community mentee (Mario Atencio), and the Diné-centered mentors (Drs. David Begay and David Tsosie); we thank them for their involvement and guidance throughout the research process. We are also thankful for the support of the University of New Mexico College of Education and Human Sciences and Center for Participatory Research within the College of Population Health.

FUNDING

The authors disclosed receipt of the following financial support for the research, authorship, and/or publication of this book chapter supported by the University of New Mexico (UNM) Transdisciplinary Research, Equity and Engagement Center for Advancing Behavioral Health funded by the National Institute of Minority Health and Health Disparities (U54 MD004811). Support for use of the Community Engagement Survey by the UNM Engage for Equity Team within the Center for Participatory Research was funded by the National Institute of Nursing Research (R01NR015241).

REFERENCES CITED

Becenti-Pigman, B., K. White, B. Bowman, N. L. Palmanteer-Holder, and B. Duran. 2008. "Research Policies, Process, and Protocol: The Navajo Nation Research Review Board." In *Community-Based Participatory Research for Health: From Process to Outcomes*, 2nd ed., edited by M. Minkler and N. Wallerstein, 441–45. San Francisco: Jossey-Bass.

Belone, L. 2010. "An Examination of Communicative Dialectical Tensions and Paradoxes Encountered by Native American Researchers in the Field and in the Academy." PhD diss., University of New Mexico, Albuquerque.

Belone, L., J. E. Lucero, B. Duran, G. Tafoya, E. A. Baker, D. Chan, C. Chang, E. Greene-Moton, M. A. Kelley, and N. Wallerstein. 2016. "Community-Based Participatory Research Conceptual Model: Community Partner Consultation and Face Validity." *Qualitative Health Research* 26 (1): 117–35.

Belone, L., A. Orosco, E. Damon, W. Smith-McNeal, R. Rae, M. L. Sherpa, O. Myers, A. Omeh, and N. Wallerstein. 2017. "The Piloting of a Culturally Centered American Indian Family Prevention: A CBPR Partnership Between Mescalero Apache and the University of New Mexico." *Public Health Reviews* 38 (30). https://doi.org/10.1186/s40985-017-0076-1.

Belone, L., R. Rae, K. A. Hirchak, B. Cohoe-Belone, A. Orosco, K. Shendo, and N. Wallerstein. 2020. "Dissemination of an American Indian Culturally Centered Community-Based Participatory Research Family Listening Program: Implications for Global Indigenous Well-Being." *Genealogy* 4 (4): 99. https://doi.org/10.3390/genealogy4040099.

Belone, L., J. Tosa, K. Shendo, A. Toya, K. Straits, G. Tafoya, R. Rae, E. Noyes, D. Bird, and N. Wallerstein. 2016. "Community-Based Participatory Research for Co-Creating Interventions with Native Communities: A Partnership Between the

University of New Mexico and the Pueblo of Jemez." In *Evidence-Based Psychological Practice with Ethnic Minorities: Culturally Informed Research and Clinical Strategies*, edited by N. Zane, G. Bernal, and F. T. L. Leong, 199–220. Washington, D.C.: American Psychological Association.

Blue Bird Jernigan, V., T. Jacob, T. C. R. Team, and D. Styne. 2015. "The Adaptation and Implementation of a Community-Based Participatory Research Curriculum to Build Tribal Research Capacity." *American Journal of Public Health* 105 (S3): S424–32.

Chandanabhumma, P., B. M. Duran, J. C. Peterson, C. R. Pearson, J. G. Oetzel, M. J. Dutta, and N. B. Wallerstein. 2020. "Space Within the Scientific Discourse for the Voice of the Other? Expressions of Community Voice in the Scientific Discourse of Community-Based Participatory Research." *Health Communication* 35 (5): 616–27.

Emerson, L. 2014. "Diné Culture, Decolonization, and the Politics of Hózhǫ́" In *Diné Perspectives: Reclaiming and Revitalizing Navajo Thought*, edited by L. Lee, 49–67. Tucson: University of Arizona Press.

Hicks, S., B. Duran, N. Wallerstein, M. Avila, L. Belone, J. Lucero, M. Magarati, et al. 2012. "Evaluating Community-Based Participatory Research to Improve Community-Partnered Science and Community Health." *Progress in Community Health Partnerships: Research, Education, and Action* 6 (3): 289–311.

Israel, B. A., E. Eng, A. J. Schulz, and E. A. Parker, eds. 2013. *Methods for Community-Based Participatory Research for Health*. 2nd ed. San Francisco: Jossey-Bass.

Kahn-John, M., and M. Koithan. 2015. "Living in Health, Harmony, and Beauty: The Diné (Navajo) Hózhó Wellness Philosophy." *Global Advances in Health and Medicine* 4 (3): 24–30.

Shavers, V. L., P. Fagan, D. Lawrence, W. McCaskill-Stevens, P. McDonald, D. Browne, D. McLinden, M. Christian, and E. Trimble. 2005. "Barriers to Racial/Ethnic Minority Application and Competition for NIH Research Funding." *Journal of the National Medical Association* 97 (8): 1063–77.

Tuhiwai-Smith, L. 2005. *Decolonizing Methodologies: Research and Indigenous Peoples*. London: Zed Books.

Wallerstein, N. B., and B. Duran. 2006. "Using Community-Based Participatory Research to Address Health Disparities." *Health Promotion Practice* 7: 312–23.

Wallerstein, N., M. Muhammad, S. Sanchez-Youngman, P. Rodriguez Espinosa, M. Avila, E. A. Baker, S. Barnett, et al. 2019. "Power Dynamics in Community-Based Participatory Research: A Multiple-Case Study Analysis of Partnering Contexts, Histories, and Practices." *Health Education and Behavior* 46 (S1): 19S–32S. https://doi.org/10.1177/1090198119852998.

Wallerstein, N., J. G. Oetzel, B. Duran, M. Magarati, C. Pearson, L. Belone, J. Davis, et al. 2019. "Culture-Centeredness in Community-Based Participatory Research: Contributions to Health Education Intervention Research." *Health Education Research* 34 (4): 372–88.

Walters, K. L., M. Johnson-Jennings, S. Stroud, S. Rasmus, B. Charles, S. John, J. Allen, et al. 2018. "Growing from Our Roots: Strategies for Developing Culturally Grounded Health Promotion Interventions in American Indian, Alaska Native, and Native Hawaiian Communities." *Prevention Science* 21:54–64.

Walters, K. L., and J. M. Simoni. 2009. "Decolonizing Strategies for Mentoring American Indians and Alaska Natives in HIV and Mental Health Research." *American Journal of Public Health* 99 (S1): S71–S76. https://doi.org/10.2105/AJPH.2008 .136127.

Werito, V. 2014. "Understanding Hózhǫ́ to Achieve Critical Consciousness: A Contemporary Diné Interpretation of the Philosophical Principles of Hózhǫ́." In *Diné Perspectives: Revitalizing and Reclaiming Navajo Thought*, edited by L. Lee, 25–38. Tucson: University of Arizona Press.

Werito, V., and L. Belone. 2021. "Research from a *Diné*-Centered Perspective and the Development of a Community-Based Partnership." *Health Education and Behavior* 48 (3): 361–70. https://doi.org/10.1177/10901981211011926.

PART II

TRIBAL/DISTRICT LEVEL AND UNIVERSITY PROGRAMS

Tribal Sovereignty and Self-Determination in Education
and University/Tribal/Community Partnerships

CHAPTER 7

WHAT DOES IT MEAN TO BE EDUCATED?

KELSEY DAYLE JOHN

I AM CONSISTENTLY faced with the questions, Why do I do what I do, what we do? Why do we read and write? Why do we go to universities to learn something we should be learning from our grandparents, our land, or our horses? Where does all this "theory" intersect with our reality as Indigenous peoples? Wouldn't I rather be riding horses than sitting inside a classroom? And how do we have a voice as our most authentic selves when we feel pressure to use the words and tools of our colonizers? These questions were forced out of my periphery and became the focal point of my daily life when I moved back home to Diné Bikéyah for my dissertation partnership. They are branches of one big question that has always lingered in the back of mind, in classes and libraries, during discussions and lectures, and has probably always set the tone of every paper I have ever written. That is, *what does it mean to be educated?*

I came home to the Navajo Nation as an odd type of Navajo transplant. I am Diné and grew up in Oklahoma and lived in upstate New York for nine years attending two predominantly white universities. As a kid, I would spend summer and winter vacations making the long drives out to Teec Nos Pos with my family. It took us fourteen hours to cross the rolling prairies that turned into dry mesa deserts. The landscapes were as different as the worldviews between my two worlds. I always knew when we were about to turn off to my grandparents' place because the power line crosses from the north side of the highway over to the south. The washboard county road would rattle our truck as we made our way toward the security light hovering over an old oil rig. This is Tsé'at'a', or "Between the Rocks." Even though these trips were only a couple times a year, they made a big impact on my life and shaped my worldview because I saw from another perspective that was both mine and different from mine at the same time. From here, I learned to be comfortable sliding in and out of different ways of being and worlds.

Years later, inside the same walls where my *nalí man* (paternal grandfather) would tease me as a little girl, he spoke to me with words as strong as his physical body. Language was never our barrier even though I struggled to sound out words in my own Native language. He talked to me about language during my research and told me how important it is to learn to speak both ways: the Navajo way and the Bilagáana (white) way. He and I both knew that language and speaking were more than just tonal sounds, but rather are all the ways that narrate a person's being. When I was little, I understood him most by observing his actions. My dad and he would work from sunrise until sundown, in the cold or the heat, usually building something to benefit the family, the animals, or the land. They embodied a kind of strength and grounding I did not see in men anywhere else. My nalí man was a deep type of intelligent and perceptive that made you feel like he could see into your soul or your future, which is why when he spoke about education (both formal and informal), I listened.

There has always been a push for my family to become educated. We value it, highly, but for reasons more complex than just money or status. Education is a way for us to say "we're as good or can do it better" because of who we are and what has been given to us as Diné. For us, the value of education is about making connections and not separations—being a bridge and an advocate for our people. University education never made us less Navajo; it made us more Navajo. This is because education has always been about more than the Western schooling structure. It is in the motions and practices of Diné life away from the university. It is about braiding together what others might think is contradictory, just like my grandfather encouraged: learn how to speak in both ways, because it does not split you, it connects you. What we are given as Diné is a gift that helps us succeed as unique persons in any situation because it is in our worldview. We know the colonial roots of schooling, but because of those who have walked before us (in this case my father and grandfather), we have the power to make education our own again.

My grandfather's words weave their way in and out of every paper I write, every class I teach, and every project I start because they are found not only in words and thoughts, but in motions and movements. I ended up in upstate New York in a graduate program focused on social justice and philosophy of education. Even though I wrote about home all the time, I could not be farther from it. After many attempts, reading other people's philosophies and realizing they would never fit, I started to remember my way of knowing. I made an intentional change to reflect the theoretical shift in my mind. This is how I came to be home at twenty-five years old, with a project and the question, What does it mean to be educated?

I ended up back on the Navajo Nation because I knew the land would guide and teach me. I prioritized land, language, and family during a summer where I worked to form a dissertation question that broke away from sterile academic reproductions and instead tried to write a story that reflected the complexities of my lingering question. I knew if I wanted to work in relationship with my community, I needed to be home and come to a place of knowing my place as a Diné researcher. I also knew that in order for research to be meaningful, it must be a part of something larger than myself, and finding my place was essential to the core of the question, What does it mean to be educated?

Even though my time in graduate school was challenging and I often felt like I didn't fit, I valued this time and used it as a way to think deeply about who I was, where I was from, and what my reasons were for pursuing this education. I eventually became comfortable admitting that education is not about me, but about what I can do for my community. So, I began to ask, who am I in relationship to my community? How do I reframe my priorities and think about theories and skills as tools rather than foundations? For example, how can I use scholarly writing as a way to advocate for my people? Or how do I use my degree and platform to help other Native American students who also want to pursue the question, What does it mean to be educated? And finally, since I study education, how can I tell the stories of how Diné are already experts in education and research? I started out on the Nation as a learner, not a researcher. I participated in language and culture classes and attended community events, feeling like there was so much for me to catch up on. At times, I had to set aside the theories I had formed in the New York classroom. Instead, I would draw from stories and memories to make meaning of my day.

There were a few questions people asked me over and over again: first, what are you going to do with this research? And second, how do you reconcile being half Navajo and not growing up on the reservation? At first, these questions hurt; they hit me like a blow to my identity. Then I learned to take them in and really think about how I would answer: Who am I? Where do I come from? With what I have, what is my place as a community researcher? And even though I might not see myself in a fraction of blood quantum, I *was* raised outside the community and this has given me a different set of lenses—for better or for worse. I was also consistently reminded that schooling, graduate school, and doctorate programs can't teach you everything because they filter out and prioritize a certain type of knowledge, and even when people in academia push back on that, it's hard to break down the barriers. This is because schooling has long been a tool to erase the Nativeness from our people, to teach us English, Christianity, and settler culture (Brayboy 2005; Grande 2004; Smith 2012). Recovering from this foundation is neither a simple nor quick process. But I have always seen myself in this confusing slew of overlapping tensions; it is comfortable for me.

Because I did not grow up speaking Navajo, I learned that I fit in as a Navajo in different ways, mostly physical movements and embodiments I picked up from living close to the land. Two parts of my life that have always connected my family to place (whether we are on the Navajo Nation or not) are running and horses. For all the ways I did not fit, I learned to think about philosophies of education that are embedded in traditional movements and ways of being like horsemanship and running. For example, I spend much of my time "in relationship" (or what some might call training) with my horse Bambi. This educational process is one I practice through the groundedness that Diné are horse people with instructions on how to be in right relationship to horses. The verbal sounds of "Sa'ah Naagháí Bik'eh Hózhóón" might not trigger meaning for me, but watching somebody train a horse using a Diné philosophy does. Because of this, my dissertation research was about collecting horse narratives from various community members as a way to connect traditional Diné horse knowledge with the tribal university. This is an ongoing project that aims to reframe education with the priorities of tribal universities and Native education/research as a practice that reflects the integrity of Diné worldviews embedded in our original education structures. I interviewed Diné folks about their knowledge of horses and how they understand it as education. In our conversations, we spoke about how the tribal university could address the needs of the surrounding community—both human and nonhuman. The most important part of my research was learning how to make connections between the contradictory; for example, how to connect university education with the Navajo horse world. How can education help us reflect, remember, heal, and preserve our ways of knowing and being by centering Diné education priorities? In all this, I centered on the horse because the horse is a healer for our people. Horses always bring us good things. Horse knowledges are tricky, though, because of the settler colonial world that tribal communities must navigate. A slew of policies including livestock reductions, forced removals, and grazing management have affected my community's relationship to horses, and so part of educating ourselves includes healing from settler colonial trauma.

During my fieldwork, I noticed there was a desire in the community for more spaces to share and learn horse knowledge. I recognized a passion and love for horses shared by most Diné. I observed that this love was a good and powerful thing. In November 2018, I worked with different horse knowers from around the community to put together a conference at Navajo Technical University. The aim of the conference was to center the sacredness of the horse in the tribal university space and to start breaking down some of the barriers between academic and nonacademic ways of knowing. We invited speakers and knowers from different educational backgrounds and areas of the reservation and artfully mixed these ways of knowing in the unique tribal university space. I love the tribal university because in many ways it resembles universities all over the United States, but in other ways, it is completely unique. This is an educational and dialogue space that will continue on for future years.

During the same academic year, I was asked to be an instructor for the School of Diné Studies at Navajo Technical University. I taught a course on colonization and decolonization and Diné gender and identity. In the beginning, I struggled with teaching for Diné studies because I am not fluent in Navajo, and I have a set of knowledges and lenses I felt were not meaningful for my students. My students would often ask me the same questions I asked myself when we read academic theories like, Why is this important? Why doesn't this person say this in a straightforward way? What does this have to do with our struggles here on Navajo land? In my pedagogy, I never tried to force theories into the minds of my students but tried to have dialogues about why these theories are important tools that we, as autonomous peoples, can take or leave depending on the situation. We read a collection of almost entirely Indigenous folks who wrote about the violences of settler colonialism, but more importantly, share with us how their communities heal (Brayboy 2005; Deer 2015; Deloria 2003; Grande 2004; Hubbard 2014; John 2018; Kovach 2010; Tall-Bear 2013; Tuck and Yang 2013).

I taught about Indigenous scholarship as a collective of storytellers working to share our priorities in the university not only to create a safe place for Indigenous students to land but as a way to share with non-Native communities and to protect what has been given to us. I always told my students to think about citations as a form of communal storytelling rather than a justification of our knowledges. I challenged them to write about their lives, their knowledges, and their communities by zooming in and out on local and global connections. We learned together to develop a language that was not just "academic" but was our own, even at times making up words to describe our unique encounters with settler colonialism. Together we would follow tangents and talk about topics other courses might consider "nonacademic." The tribal university was where we could work through our hesitations about education and develop our voices because we already have them from all the education in our life (whether that's in a school setting, in a horse corral, or on the mesa).

As it goes, my academic path takes many different turns, but the goal is for education to be both academic and nonacademic and to gracefully dismantle the separations between these two ways of knowing. My goal as an educator is to promote any type of learning that heals and to fight rigorously for creating harmony in the lives of Indigenous learners. In the future, I see this as a lifelong project that continuously centers horses and land as teachers and healers for Indigenous learners. I envision future possibilities for collaboration between tribal universities and the surrounding Native community as well as partnering non-tribal universities.

Just like my physical move home resembled my priorities (to leave the university and return home), I see all movements across space as intellectually complex thoughts and communications. Two years later, I parted from my time as a researcher on the Nation and now think about the next set of movements I will make to narrate my priorities. I am a professor and struggled with the decision to leave teaching at a tribal university and move to a larger public university in Arizona just like many students might struggle with their decision to leave home for school or for a job. I still feel this when I ask myself, When will I return to my community? And if I am not on the land, and not working in Navajo institutions, am I still a meaningful member of the community? But my grandfather's last words to me helped me see that movements across space (away from home or back home), whether for the summer or for years, are our way to embody priorities. Before his passing, he said, "No matter where you go, you will always be Diné. Because you have your clans. Clans do not change because they derive from places of land. You could rename the place where Tłááshchi'i people are from, but it will always be that Tłááshchi'i." Clans originate from the Earth, from the land; it does not matter how many times they rename the place where we originate, it will always be the same place. Our identity is as strong as the land. In essence, he reminded me that no matter where you go, you will be Navajo, just as the land will never not be Navajo land no matter what we do to it.

This chapter is for any learner whether they are in formal schooling or not, on the reservation or off. I write in hope that education will be many things beyond schooling and that value systems will shift to accept different ways of knowing not as contradictory but as melody.

REFERENCES CITED

Brayboy, B. M. J. 2005. "Toward a Tribal Critical Race Theory in Education." *Urban Review* 37 (5): 425–46.

Deer, S. 2015. *The Beginning and End of Rape: Confronting Sexual Violence in Native America*. Minneapolis: University of Minnesota Press.

Deloria, V., Jr. 2003. *God Is Red: A Native View of Religion*. Golden, CO: Fulcrum.

Grande, S. 2004. *Red Pedagogy: Native American Social and Political Thought*. Lanham, MD: Rowman and Littlefield.

Hubbard, T. 2014. "Buffalo Genocide in Nineteenth-Century North America: 'Kill, Skin, and Sell.'" In *Colonial Genocide in Indigenous North America*, edited by A. Laban Hinton, A. Woolford, and J. Benvenuto, 292–305. Durham, NC: Duke University Press.

John, K. D. 2018. "Rez Ponies and Confronting Sacred Junctures in Decolonizing and Indigenous Education." In *Indigenous and Decolonizing Studies in Education: Mapping the Long View*, edited by L. T. Smith, E. Tuck, and K. W. Yang, 50–61. New York: Routledge.

Kovach, M. E. 2010. *Indigenous Methodologies: Characteristics, Conversations, and Contexts*. Toronto: University of Toronto Press.

Smith, L. T. 2012. *Decolonizing Methodologies: Research and Indigenous Peoples*. London: Zed Books.

TallBear, K. 2013. *Native American DNA: Tribal Belonging and the False Promise of Genetic Science*. Minneapolis: University of Minnesota Press.

Tuck, E., and K. W Yang. 2012. "Decolonization Is Not a Metaphor." *Decolonization: Indigeneity, Education, and Society* 1 (1). https://jps.library.utoronto.ca/index.php/des/article/view/18630/15554.

CHAPTER 8

THE CORN POLLEN MODEL

A Holistic Pathway to Leadership, Education, and Well-Being

SHAWN SECATERO

THE CORN POLLEN PATH

You are created as a seed that was planted in our sacred Mother Earth to honor your purpose, mind, body, and relations. Honor your roots, grow your leaves of knowledge, stand strong as a cornstalk, and sprout your beautiful tassels for your people. Always remember who you are, where you are from, and where you are going in life. Create and continue your legacy by following the corn pollen path through education, well-being, and leadership.

The Indigenous-based Corn Pollen Model, or "At'aa' da'diin baa' Hane'" in the Navajo language, is a holistic framework that evolved from my qualitative dissertation study, "Beneath Our Sacred Minds, Hands, and Hearts: Stories of Persistence and Success Among American Indian Graduate and Professional Students" (Secatero 2009). The results from my study indicated that honoring the holistic connections of spiritual, mental, physical, and social well-being contributed to overall success for graduate participants in this study. Furthermore, their success stories and determination ignited my interest in creating a holistic education and leadership model that would inspire and help other future scholars learn about the importance of holistic education, leadership, and well-being.

In this chapter, I introduce the holistic leadership concepts of the Corn Pollen Model that relate to our overall well-being. In addition, I will introduce the evolution of the model in four stages, four main pillars, and twelve sub-pillars, and the implications for leadership and education.

I was very fortunate to be raised traditionally on the Canoncito Navajo Reservation and grew up participating in ceremonies that involved the sacred use of corn pollen. My father, the late Leon Secatero, told me about the importance of corn pollen and prayer each morning:

> Each morning, you face east before the sun rises and pray to the holy ones by blessing yourself with corn pollen. You begin by sprinkling corn pollen on top of your head, forehead, heart, limbs, and feet. This practice honors our holy beings as they recognize your sacred existence in this world. You are protected and blessed. (pers. comm., 2008)

HOLISTIC LEADERSHIP AND WELL-BEING

The concept of holistic leadership serves as the focus of my research as an associate professor at the University of New Mexico (UNM). Dhiman (2019, 275) describes holistic leadership as "a moral and spiritual journey whose guiding compass is found within a leader's soul. The first step begins with self-knowledge." As leaders and educators, we must create a vision within ourselves before progressing into action and simultaneously acknowledging our balance through well-being. According to the Institute for Education Leadership (2020), well-being serves as a holistic balance among individuals:

> Well-being is a positive sense of self, spirit and belonging that we feel when our cognitive, emotional, social, spiritual and physical needs are being met. It is supported through equity and respect for our diverse identities and strengths. Well-being is about helping school and system leaders become resilient, so that they can make positive and healthy choices to support learning and achievement both now and in the future.

The sacred symbol of corn in Navajo cultural lifeways serves as a holistic symbol of success for all students in education, well-being, and leadership. The symbolic roots of the corn serve as our spiritual connections to the earth through cultural, linguistic, and artistic well-being. The corn leaves represent our knowledge systems that correlate to mental well-being. Additionally, the embedded pillars of emotional, intellectual, and technical well-being further promote the concepts of mindfulness and thinking processes. The corn stalk represents our third quadrant, which refers to physical well-being, which relates to self-care and health. This bonding strength of physical well-being refers to additional sub-pillars, including environmental, cyclical, and medicinal well-being. Finally, the corn tassel serves as a symbol of our social, professional, economic, and political well-being pillars. These examples of relationships, professional well-being, economics, and political attributes represent a holistic pathway to honoring leadership and education.

PLANTING OF THE CORN POLLEN MODEL

The Corn Pollen Model began to grow its seed in 1997 and progressed through four stages to become a four-quadrant model consisting of spiritual, mental, physical, and social well-being. As part of growth and change, the corn continued its growth by adding twelve sub-pillars through the nurturing of elders, Native scholars, and international and non-Native resources. The Corn Pollen Model followed its own path of "Sa'ah Naaghái Bik'eh Hózhǫ́ǫ́n," or Navajo traditional living system of harmony. My reflection is based on Diné College's (2020) Navajo philosophy, which includes the four sacred concepts of thinking, planning, living, and assuring.

STAGE ONE: NITSÁHÁKEES (THINKING)

The Corn Pollen Model began its development from 1997 to 2000 during my doctoral research journey when interviewing Canoncito Navajo elders about their perceptions of well-being. Their responses planted the holistic seeds of spiritual, mental, physical, and social well-being attributes. Spiritual well-being is referred to as "Hodiyingo," which provides people with purpose and balance. Mental well-being is called "Bini'" in the Dine' language and includes mind and thinking processes; physical well-being is referred to as "A'tsiis," which includes self-care and developmental changes. Social well-being refers to relationships and community and is often referred to as "K'é" in the Navajo language. These basic four pillars of well-being are strongly connected in harmony to promote a holistic framework for well-being. In reference to the corn model, these four pillars consist of a developmental phase of learning and growing and serve as the "roots" of our existence.

STAGE TWO: NAHAT'Á (PLANNING)

As I was developing the four main well-being pillars based on information from my elders, I applied these concepts to research and data collection for the second stage of my research that evolved into planning my dissertation. I interviewed twenty-three American Indian scholars from across the country from various tribes who had attained a master's or professional degree with various majors. My research focused on this question: As a Native American graduate student, how did you succeed and persist at the graduate level? My study participants also completed an online survey, which contained questions on spiritual, mental, physical, and social well-being. In addition, seven of my study participants wrote personal stories about their pathway to success and provided much needed insight for potential American Indian students who wanted to attain higher degrees. As a result of my research, I added four additional well-being pillars as suggested by my research participants, which included cultural well-being (identity), emotional well-being (heart), environmental well-being (place), and professional well-being (goals).

STAGE THREE: IINÁ (LIVING)

The living of life component was added as the third stage of the Corn Pollen Model in 2010–2012 by combining both Western ways of knowing and Indigenous education. I continued to think beyond Indigenous research by identifying holistic education concepts such as Gardner's (2006) "multiple intelligences," Bloom's taxonomy (Anderson and Sosniak 1994), the Learning Pyramid (Lalley and Miller 2007), Washington

State University's (2020) "Wellbeing Online" site, and wellness resources such as Rath and Harter (2010). From these sources, I added the concepts of technical well-being that include future planning, cyclical well-being that addresses time and change in our everyday lives, economic well-being that highlights financial management and capital, and political well-being that acknowledges leadership and trust in our everyday lives. The Corn Pollen Model continued to grow with twelve sub-pillars, and I decided to add an international perspective.

STAGE FOUR: SIHASIN (ASSURING)

The final stage of the Corn Pollen Model focused on the Navajo concept of reassurance that my model was continuing its growth to survive in the research and traditional worlds. My research collection continued to grow and blossom in 2013. I presented the Corn Pollen Model at several international conferences such as the World Indigenous Peoples Conference in Education (WIPCE), the Nga Pae O Te Maramatanga Maori Research for Excellence in New Zealand, and aboriginal education programs in Australia to provide me further guidance. As I continued to collect more information from an international perspective, I added artistic well-being, which acknowledges giftedness, and intellectual well-being, which is strongly related to wisdom and character. Also, there needed to be a healing and resiliency concept that I labeled medicinal well-being. Several conference attendees stressed the importance of language revitalization, so I included linguistic well-being.

It is important to note that the Corn Pollen Model can be utilized by all nations and nationalities as a curriculum model to learn about spiritual, mental, physical, and social well-being. The Corn Pollen Model continues to be revised and developed as we continue to grow in education, leadership, and well-being. I would like to focus on Canoncito Navajo–based teachings from the well-being model that include (1) honoring your roots through spiritual well-being, (2) growing your leaves of knowledge as part of mental well-being, (3) standing strong as a cornstalk to illustrate physical well-being, and (4) sprouting your tassels of success for your people that correlates to social well-being. I will share the symbols, key terms, strengths, and challenges of each of the four main pillars along with the twelve sub-pillars.

HONORING YOUR ROOTS (SPIRITUAL WELL-BEING)

The spiritual well-being quadrant is connected to creating a vision or purpose in one's life, which also connects to cultural well-being (identity), linguistic well-being (language/voice), and artistic well-being (giftedness). Among Navajo people, the concept of "Sa'ah Naagháí Bik'eh Hózhǫ́ǫ́n" (SNBH) is strongly associated with spiritual well-being, as Lewton writes, "SNBH encompasses complex ideas about the spatiotemporal environment, spiritual beings, and people's relationships with these elements. Harmony or balance requires the establishment and maintenance of proper relationships guided by principles such as respect, reverence, kindness, and cooperation" (2000, 479).

SPIRITUAL (EAST): HODIYINGO (PURPOSE; CORN POLLEN)

Examples of spiritual well-being include visionary and spiritual leadership, which include such Indigenous-based strengths as ceremony, hope, reassurance, daily prayer, observance of sacred events, and balancing the modern and traditional ways of life. The challenges of spiritual well-being include loss of family, death, and lack of self-actualization and self-worth.

CULTURAL WELL-BEING: BI'IL'OOLIIL (IDENTITY)

Cultural well-being refers to the pattern of hands—there are no two alike in the world, which defines an individual as unique: "Cultural well-being is about having the freedom to practice your own culture, and to belong to a cultural group. Cultural well-being comes from being valued for the differences that define us and our beliefs, our history, and our roots" (https://www.etsu.edu/wellness/dimensionswellness.php). Multicultural and cross-cultural leadership are positive practices of cultural well-being, which promotes the sense of belonging, inclusiveness, knowledge of clan groups, kinship, appreciation for diversity, and critical race theory. The challenges of cultural well-being include loss of culture, history, norms, confusion of identity, lack of maturity, racism, lack of appreciation of diversity, and criticizing differences.

LINGUISTIC WELL-BEING: BIZAAD

"Bizaad" also includes the voice of the drum, which serves as a heart-beat of language through sacred songs; without these songs, an individual society can no longer exist. Linguistic well-being is a new term that I define as patterns of thought and communication that are tied to behavior, belief systems, cultures, and our reality. It also includes honoring voices that preserve languages. One example of leadership relating to linguistic well-being is oratory leadership, which refers to a person who knows how to bring people together through voice, reasoning, and bilingualism. Reading, writing, speaking, listening, oral history, Native language preservation, bilingualism, and voice are a few examples of linguistic well-being. The challenges of linguistic well-being include loss of Native language, lack of respect for bilingualism, negativity, and use of profanity.

ARTISTIC WELL-BEING: NA'ACH'AAH (GIFT/CRAFT)

The symbol of artistic well-being is connected to the sacred basket that honors the circle of giving among people. I would define artistic well-being as honoring the past, present, and future through the creative expression of giftedness. In the art of leadership, artistic well-being can be rooted to an individual who is a powerful influence on others' personalities, belief systems, and cultures. Examples of artistic well-being include giftedness, singing, film development, media documentation, arts and crafts, dancing, traditions, pedagogy, and mastery learning. The challenges of artistic well-being include lack of pride in work, giving up, anxiety, and lack of patience or understanding.

GROW YOUR LEAVES OF KNOWLEDGE (MENTAL WELL-BEING)

In the mental well-being quadrant, the pillars connect to thinking or cognition skills that include emotional well-being, or heart; intellectual well-being, or wisdom; and technical well-being, or future skills needed to promote wellness. As Benally (1992) writes,

The essence of Dine philosophy is holism and the goal it sets for life is peace and harmony. By balancing the four cardinal areas of Navajo knowledge (life direction, self-reliance, family relationships, and reverence) the individual will develop sound beliefs and values and be prepared to make responsible decisions. He will develop knowledge and skills so that he will be able to provide for his family, demonstrate good leadership within the family and community, and retain a sense of reverence for all things, both those on the earth and in the heavens. There is a great central focus where all forms of knowledge converge. In Navajo, this point of convergence is the synthesis of knowledge obtained from the cardinal points that find expression in appreciation, reverence, and love for harmony.

MENTAL WELL-BEING: BINI

The leaves of knowledge are symbolic for mental-well-being, which I define as the ability to comprehend thinking processes, learning strategies, and stimulations of the mind. Examples of mental well-being are thinking, critical analysis, learning styles, creativity, problem solving, multitasking, and understanding. The challenges of mental well-being include mental abuse, fear, doubt, and negative outlook on life.

EMOTIONAL WELL-BEING: BA'ANI (ARROWHEAD)

The arrowhead is a sacred part of well-being, which relates to your heart and love. Emotional well-being is recognizing and understanding the heart of wellness through emotions and healthy lifestyles, caring for others, and showing compassion for less fortunate living beings. Examples of emotional well-being are happiness, giving to others, anger/stress management, positive attitude, love, affection, caring, friendship, and approachability. The challenges of emotional well-being include fear, powerlessness, victimization, jealousy, anger, blame, boredom, and revenge.

INTELLECTUAL WELL-BEING: NITSÁHÁKEES (TOBACCO)

The practice of sharing wisdom involves the sacred use of tobacco among elders. Intellectual well-being can be defined as being open and responsive to new ideas, critical thinking, and learning from elders and knowledge keepers. It is also strongly tied to character development and building a positive reputation. Examples of intellectual well-being include experience, character, mentoring, respect, responsibility, rigor, insight, relevance, instinct, elder teachings, advisement, and knowledge keeping. The challenges of intellectual well-being include lack of confidence, bad attitude, bad judgment, and disrespecting elders.

TECHNICAL WELL-BEING: BEE'NANISH (CELESTIAL BEINGS)

The stars and celestial beings help guide critical thinking and into the future of the unknown. Technical well-being can be further defined as learning to navigate technology, planning ahead, and accepting change by building knowledge. Examples of technical well-being include technology and planning, forecasting, science, math, computers, netiquette, and giving back to future generations. The challenges of technical well-being are as follows: closed-mindedness, fear of technology, negative outlook on community, lack of planning or initiative, frustration, and no positive outlook on the future.

STAND STRONG AS A CORNSTALK (PHYSICAL WELL-BEING): IINÁ (LIVING)

The physical well-being quadrant is related to the body and includes environmental well-being, or sense of place; cyclical well-being, or honoring time/change; and medicinal well-being, which is needed for healing purposes. In relation to the Corn Pollen Model, the stalk must stand strong to support the leaves, roots, and tassels for growth. You cannot lead if you are not well, and physical stamina is necessary for leadership. Kahn-John (2010) further contends that physical well-being relates to the concept of "Hózhǫ́" by stating,

> Hózhó is a Diné word portraying a supreme state of Diné being, a balanced and beautiful way of living—wellness and health. The word Hózhó reflects a theme of constant and respectful relationship with self, others, the Diné Holy Ones, and the environment. The Diné people who have achieved Hózhó in their lives have relied upon an elusive inner strength

and constant mindfulness that is made up of certain behaviors, attitudes, beliefs, and ritual spiritual practices that may be unique to Diné culture. Some literature alludes to the significance of Hózhó because it is a key to a life of health, harmony, and well-being.

Examples of physical well-being include proper diet, exercise, health awareness, drug and alcohol prevention, hygiene, and family medical history. The challenges of physical well-being are physical abuse, lack of self-care, alcohol and drug abuse, learned helplessness, negative self-image, and bad diet.

ENVIRONMENTAL WELL-BEING: KÉYAH (LAND)

The sense of place is very important, such as having a safe living environment or home. The symbol for environmental well-being is a hogan, or living quarters. I refer to environmental well-being as honoring our environment by respecting all living beings, Mother Earth, and Father Sky. It also includes creating a safe home, school, work, and community environment for future generations. Examples of environmental well-being include travel, geography, honoring Mother Earth and Father Sky, sacred site preservation, protecting all living things, climate change awareness, and cleanliness. The challenges of environmental well-being include pollution, lack of safety, destroying nature, no respect for living things, and lack of resources for the people.

CYCLICAL WELL-BEING: NINAHAHI

"Ninahahi" refers to honoring time, change, seasons, and development. The sacred symbol for cyclical well-being is a calendar. Every nation has a calendar to monitor time and change, which is also important in leadership that cultivates the planning process for community survival. I would define cyclical well-being as understanding the concepts of time and change through stages of development, which includes learning patience and creating positive outcomes for a group of people. Examples of cyclical well-being include time management, maturation processes, rites of passage, birth, childhood, adulthood, elder status, responsiveness to change, and patience. The challenges of cyclical well-being include lack of patience, tardiness, lack of forecasting, no respect for the seasons, and no vision for the future of community.

MEDICINAL WELL-BEING: AZEE'

The medicine bundle is the symbol for medicinal well-being, which can also include forgiveness, balance, and resiliency. I would posit that medicinal well-being is the ability to heal ourselves from life obstacles and challenges to restore our mind, body, and spirit. This includes restoration of self, restructuring our life, reflection on good things, and reshaping our surroundings. Examples of medicinal well-being include knowledge of medicinal herbs, rest, relaxation, rejuvenation, counseling, talking circles, self-restoration, and health awareness. The challenges of medicinal well-being include trauma, abuse, assault, drama, and destruction of living creatures, plants, and sacred sites.

SPROUT BEAUTIFUL TASSELS FOR YOUR PEOPLE (SOCIAL WELL-BEING)

In the final quadrant, social well-being correlates to honoring relations to embody professional well-being, or goals; economic well-being, or maintaining stability; and political well-being, which connects leadership attributes to lifelong learning. Social well-being has been defined as "a person's state of mind, relationship with the world around them, and the fulfilment they get from life. It can be understood as how people feel and how they function, both on a personal and a social level, and how they evaluate their lives" (Copps and Plimmer 2013). Lee (2008, 103) further describes Navajo-based practices of social well-being as self-determination and building Nationhood: "Respect and honor create interactions and relationships based on *hadine'e baa haajinizin* (having compassion for your people), *hadine'e ayoi'ojo'nih* (having love for your people), and *hadine'e hwil niliigo* (respecting your people)."

SOCIAL WELL-BEING: K'É

K'é highlights the importance of relationships such as clanship, community, and social networks. The sacred symbol of social well-being refers to corn tassels, which relate to the sacredness and heart of prayers by using corn pollen. Furthermore, corn pollen is used in a ceremony that involves the successful interactions with family and community and networking with support structures to achieve social justice. Examples of social well-being include family and extended family, collaboration, friendship circles, humor, and social justice. The challenges of social well-being include ignorance, lack of family structure, bad influences, passivity, and discrimination.

PROFESSIONAL WELL-BEING: NANISH'ISHI

"Nanish'ishi" refers to setting goals in life and achievement. A common symbol for achievement is the eagle feather, which is considered sacred for professional well-being among many Native nations. Professional well-being is achieving wellness through the enrichment of life goals, education, career aspirations, purpose, and finding happiness. Examples of professional well-being include short- and long-term goal planning, ethics, job skills, people skills, professionalism, organization, and evaluation. Challenges of professional well-being include lack of career skills, authoritative attitude, bad judgment, and no positive outlook in the community.

ECONOMIC WELL-BEING: BAAH HAA HASIN

"Baah háá hasin" refers to creating a stable life through socioeconomics and financial literacy. The ownership of livestock is an example of economic well-being, survival, and prosperity for many Native nations. I would further define economic well-being as creating a stable life though effective decision-making, nation building, savings, and improving one's socioeconomic background. Examples of economic well-being include resources, financial literacy, resource development, capital, and understanding global trends. Challenges of economic well-being include greed, nepotism, favoritism, poverty, power struggles, and materialistic wealth.

POLITICAL WELL-BEING: BINAHAT'A

The symbol of political well-being is a spear-staff, which is given to a leader by medicine people. Political well-being is developing a stronger sustainable community through positive change, service, care, trust, and giving back to your people. Prime examples of political well-being include honesty, integrity, leadership, sovereignty, self-determination, advocacy, inspirational leadership, and success. Challenges of political well-being include distrust, misuse of power, self-righteousness, and negative practices to bring down a community.

FUTURE OF THE CORN POLLEN MODEL

The Corn Pollen Model continues to evolve as a holistic-based framework for future educators, leaders, and generations to enjoy and preserve. Several educational leadership courses at UNM have integrated these concepts into their curriculum. For example, the Corn Pollen Model Framework is utilized in leadership courses such as Schools as Organizations, Leadership in a Democratic Society, and Leadership Perspectives. In addition, teacher and principal education programs such as UNM's Promoting Our Leadership, Learning, and Empowering our Nations (POLLEN), American Indian Professional Educators Collaborative (AIPEC), and Native American Leadership in Education (NALE), and the Striking Eagle Native American Invitational Academy (SENAI) have integrated the Corn Pollen Model into their educational programs such as workshops and academies. Students have developed their own sacred symbols and leadership models to demonstrate their knowledge in holistic teaching and education. In the future, the Corn Pollen Model will continue to blossom into an educational leadership curriculum as students recraft their vision of creating their beauty way path of sacred blessings, "Si'ah Naaghái Bik'eh Hózhóón."

REFERENCES CITED

Anderson, L. W., and L. A. Sosniak (editors). 1994. *Bloom's Taxonomy: A Forty-Year Retrospective*. Chicago: National Society for the Study of Education.
Benally, H. 1992. "Spiritual Knowledge for a Secular Society: Traditional Navajo Spirituality Offers Lessons for the Nation." *Tribal College* 3 (4). https://tribalcollegejournal.org/spiritual-knowledge-secular-society-traditional-navajo-spirituality-offers-lessons-nation/.

Copps, J., and D. Plimmer. 2013. "Outcomes Map: Personal and Social Well-Being." New Philanthropy Capital, London. https://www.thinknpc.org/wp-content/uploads/2018/07/Outcomes-map-well-being.pdf.

Dhiman, S. 2017. *Holistic Leadership: A New Paradigm for Today's Leaders*. New York: Palgrave Macmillan.

Diné College. 2020. "Educational Philosophy." https://www.dinecollege.edu/about_dc/educational-philosophy/.

Gardner, H. 2006. *Multiple Intelligences: New Horizons*. New York: Basic Books.

Institute for Education Leadership (Ontario). 2020. "Well-Being for Leadership." https://www.education-leadership-ontario.ca/en/resources/collaborative-learning-model/well-being-leadership.

Kahn-John, M. 2010. "Concept Analysis of Diné Hózhó: A Diné Wellness Philosophy." *Advances in Nursing Science* 33 (2): 113–25. https://doi.org/10.1097/ANS.0b013e3181dbc658.

Lalley, J. P., and R. H. Miller. 2007. "The Learning Pyramid: Does It Point Teachers in the Right Direction?" *Education* 128 (1): 64–79.

Lee, L. L. 2008. "Reclaiming Indigenous Intellectual, Political, and Geographic Space: A Path for Navajo Nationhood." *American Indian Quarterly* 32 (1): 96–110.

Lewton, E. L. 2000. "Identity and Healing in Three Navajo Religious Traditions: Sa'ah Naaghái Bik'eh Hózho." *Medical Anthropology Quarterly* 14 (4): 476.

Rath, T., and J. Harter. 2010. *Wellbeing: The Five Essential Elements*. New York: Gallup Press.

Secatero, S. 2009. "Beneath Our Sacred Minds, Hands, and Hearts: Stories of Persistence and Success Among American Indian Graduate and Professional Students." PhD diss., University of New Mexico, Albuquerque.

Washington State University. 2020. "Wellbeing Online." https://wellbeingonline.wsu.edu.

CHAPTER 9

DREAM DINÉ CHARTER SCHOOL

The First New Mexico Elementary Public Charter School
Serving the Diné

QUINTINA "TINA" DESCHENIE

Using heavy-duty needles, awls, and sinew to sew thick leather soles to buckskin, the adults formed the footwear, while the elementary students worked on the paper tracings used to make the moccasin patterns. They painted Earth illustrations on the soles and Sky illustrations on the leggings to depict Diné teachings. As she sewed, one grandmother stated, "Now I understand why moccasins are so expensive. It takes a lot of work to make them." Aside from the instructor, none in the room had ever made moccasins before. The activity was an excellent example of how sovereignty in education should work in a school classroom: intergenerational learning engaging visual, auditory, and kinesthetic modes of educational experiences.

SCARCELY ANY Diné make moccasins anymore. In the past, families taught and learned language and culture together in their homes. Ah Nee-Benham and Cooper wrote that Indigenous education "must be interdisciplinary, intercultural, and involve multiple generations from the community" (2000, 18). The Cornell University student who taught moccasin making at Dream Diné Charter School (DDCS) described

Quintina "Tina" Deschenie served as Head Administrator at Dream Diné Charter School from 2016 to 2019. The research and content of this chapter are not intended to reflect the views of the Dream Diné Charter School or its representatives. They are solely the perspectives of the author.

above had learned the skill from Diné College's Navajo Cultural Arts certificate program. Instruction on cultural topics, including making traditional regalia or crafts, was procured from paid consultants (often young people who had learned the skills from a tribal college).

COMMUNITY SELF-DETERMINATION DROVE THE SCHOOL

The DDCS founders opened the school to develop "strong, compassionate, bilingual young people who are committed to their personal and community health, wellness, relationships and progress" (https://www .dreamdine.org/who-we-are/our-dream). The school mission states: "Dream Diné Charter School is a place-based elementary school where the Diné philosophy, wisdom, history and teachings are the foundation of a dual-language, experiential curriculum" (https://www.dreamdine.org/ who-we-are/mission).

As I wrote in my dissertation, "Historically, community-based leadership that promotes a Diné cultural agenda—one centered on Diné language instruction—in public school districts serving Diné students has been extremely rare" (Deschenie 2013, 5). This has slowly changed in the New Mexico public schools that serve Navajo students: "In 2005, the Navajo Nation passed the Sovereignty in Diné Education Act (SDEA) which calls for Diné specific education to be provided to Diné students in all of the schools that serve them" (Deschenie 2013, 37). Sixteen years later, the SDEA, which supports language and culture learning, has not been fully implemented in 2021.

State-funded public charter schools are still new to Diné communities. As of 2021, there were only two in New Mexico: DDCS, serving grades K–5 in Shiprock, and Dził Ditłʼooi School of Empowerment, Action and Perseverance (DEAP), serving grades 6–10 in Navajo. Both school charters were reauthorized for second terms: DDCS in 2019 and DEAP in 2020. Both schools started as state charter schools, rather than as district charter schools; in 2021, state or district authorization are the only two options for New Mexico charter schools.

The Native American charter school movement, primarily state-funded education, is an example of self-determination whereby the schools strive to teach language and culture. Diné self-determination in education started when Rough Rock Demonstration School in 1966 and the Ramah Navajo School in 1970 were established by Diné leaders to challenge the BIA boarding school system, using federal funds available through P.L. 93-638. By perpetuating Diné language, culture, and history in the school curricula, community schools reinforce Diné traditional teachings of self-determination that are inherent to the Navajo Beauty Way teachings. While the schools are not teaching sacred prayers, it is possible, even likely, that the adults are praying at home for their children to learn and for the schools to grow.

Nine public school districts in the state serve Navajo students in 53 (of 110 total) Navajo Nation chapters (New Mexico Public Education Department 2009, 26). While public school districts make reports at local chapters, they are overseen by the state department. By contrast, DDCS utilized the Shiprock Chapter almost daily at times: as an auditorium and as a school kitchen and dining area. However, when the school's charter renewal was discussed at the Central Consolidated School District's (CCSD) board meetings, chapter representatives provided testimony both pro and con about the school. Chapter and community politics impacted the school.

DDCS has a five-member governing council (GC) that meets voluntarily monthly to develop policies, to provide oversight of the budget, and to provide direction to administration. Among the members, one had served since before the school opened and a second started soon after the school started. The GC was composed of individuals with graduate degrees, including a physician at the local Indian Health Service.

DDCS also has an active Parent Advisory Committee (PAC), whose president serves on the GC. The PAC meets monthly to discuss parent-specific needs and school programs, and hosts a monthly family night. PAC activity depends on the availability and commitment from the elected officers. During the school renewal process, PAC officers regularly attended chapter and school district meetings to represent DDCS.

A core group of families supported the school at public meetings, but it was rare for a large group of parents to do so. This may indicate general parent satisfaction with the school operations, or trust in the administration and GC to address issues, or apathy. The majority of parents supported the school through participation in classroom activities, school programs, and parent-teacher conferences.

DDCS welcomed parents and elders to volunteer at the school. Of two elders who volunteered regularly, one, a retired teacher, provided after-school tutoring in reading and math; the second preferred to work on bulletin boards rather than assist the students directly. Neither indicated interest in Diné language or culture instruction, likely due to lack of experience caused by assimilation, which generally does not value Diné culture or language. It soon became apparent that very few parents could reinforce the language and culture instruction, which only further underscored the need for the school. Parents more freely shared in the classrooms about careers, outdoor activities, and traditional food preparation or assisted with grounds upkeep.

Most families are used to how traditional public schools operate, where there is no need to advocate for a school to continue to exist, no matter how well or poorly it may do. Or their potential participation is hindered by state regulations that complicate volunteering in the schools. Even so, in their mission and goals, all Native charter schools call for active parent and community engagement.

DDCS was well supported by community organizations throughout the years. The Indian Health Service, Office of Diné Youth, and Native Vision provided physical education. The New Mexico State University Research Station and its Yeego Garden Project provided gardening and nutrition instruction, installed a greenhouse, and planted garden beds and fruit trees on campus. The Healing Circle staff provided cultural teachings. United Health provided water in drinking bottles. The Shiprock Chapter House assisted with maintaining the campus. The Farmington-based University of New Mexico (UNM) teacher education program provided student teachers to lead family learning activities. UNM and Diné College teacher education programs occasionally provided student teacher interns. Navajo Preparatory School's student service-learning groups hosted learning activities. The San Juan College Alternative Licensure program supported teachers acquiring licensure.

DDCS contracted with the CCSD for food services, participated in the district's bilingual professional development by agreement, and rented a school bus and driver for occasional field trips. The nearby Head Start school administration claimed federal funding policy limited possible collaboration. Among all the local school systems, public and federal, DDCS was the youngest school, and it operated mostly in isolation from the others.

A highlight for the school was being part of the Native American Community Academy (NACA) Inspired Schools Network (NISN). The NISN website states, "NISN supports leaders in Indigenous communities to develop a network of schools providing rigorous academic curriculum aimed at college preparation while also promoting Indigenous culture, identity, and community involvement" (http://www.nacainspiredschoolsnetwork.org/). NISN was invaluable to the school, providing grants, access to professional development, IT help, operations guidance, teacher coaching, community outreach, school reviews, and support for student assessment. NISN also convened staff of its network schools to address common goals and issues.

Since funding for start-up charter schools is limited, the school sought grants. An important source for support costs was the Kellogg Foundation. On its website, the foundation mission states that it "support[s] children, families and communities as they strengthen and create conditions that propel vulnerable children to achieve success as individuals and as contributors to the larger community and society" (https://www.wkkf.org/who-we-are/overview?#mission-vision). The Kellogg grant allowed the school to pay for administrative support costs including personnel, capacity-building, curriculum development, and technology equipment.

THE DINÉ LANGUAGE WAS A STRENGTH IN THE SCHOOL

The Diné language and culture curriculum was never significantly undermined by its place alongside the English curriculum, but student performance on the state English assessments was a constant pressure. Equal time had been allocated for English and Diné to honor the school's mission. Nevertheless, although English was the primary language of all of the households served by the school, the perception persisted that more time to teach English was needed. The fact that Diné was scarcely spoken outside of the classroom hardly translated to concern about more time being devoted to Diné instruction for better performance on the Diné language assessment. The state's priority of English language development was entrenched in the minds of parents. The teachers were also concerned, since their evaluation criteria included student performance on academic assessments.

Still, the students far outperformed any of the English language–based state assessments on the Oral Diné Language Assessment (ODLA) annually during the last three years of the first charter contract. In year five, 100 percent of the students exceeded the school charter goal: "80% of the students are to make 10% growth on the ODLA from pre- to post-test." Unfortunately, this phenomenal effort was not reflected on the state report cards, which never considered the Diné language achievement. It was a conundrum that the school received F or D grades, when assessment on 50 percent of its curriculum had earned at least an A.

Their children's learning in Diné often amazed the families. Grandparents regularly expressed pride that their grandchildren spoke and sang in Diné at home, skills they often didn't have and had not learned in their own schooling. Some parents who did not speak the language expressed disappointment at their own inabilities; fortunately, they often learned from their children.

When the CCSD initially resisted Dream Diné's charter renewal, one reason offered was that a dual language program already existed in one of its schools. The unasked question was this: *Can there be too many dual language schools in Shiprock when language loss is a threat to literally all Native American languages?* At a board meeting, district representatives also questioned whether DDCS taught religion or carried on ceremonies at the school. Citing state laws, they emphasized this could not be happening—and it wasn't. Although the school's mission is to teach Diné language and culture, the criticism inaccurately implied it was violating state law regarding religion.

There are beautiful stories about traditional Diné ways of collaboration and use of resources to develop and grow as a people. The GC had hoped that the Diné leadership on the CCSD board and administration would embrace the school. Some Diné board members did express admiration for the school's dual language curriculum, but that was subverted by their staff's singular concern with state accountability metrics. The school was described as a potential liability for the district. Some Diné representatives of the Shiprock Chapter also spoke against the school at the board meetings. It was difficult to find consistent support from the chapter and the school district.

This opposition from Diné leaders is contrary to traditional Diné leadership values as transmitted in traditional teachings and stories, such as in the following story:

> A part of the Diné Creation story recalls the selection of and the responsibilities of leaders. It is told that the wolf, the bluebird, the mountain lion, and the hummingbird were each nominated to become the leader. When each animal presented different offerings needed to sustain life—the sky, the dawn, the sunset, the night, songs, words, food—the People determined that all of them were necessary, and they were all selected to work together. (Deschenie 2013, 63)

The Navajo Nation Supreme Court, which retold this story in a case involving Navajo leadership, stated that "since beyond recorded time, the People have understood . . . that in order to survive as a People, there must be collaboration and coming together both in the community and in the leadership chosen by the People to pool skills, resources and characteristics" (Deschenie 2013, 63). Accordingly, Diné leaders should collaborate and respect one another's strengths and abilities. There is room for everyone to contribute something. If following this mode of thinking, the GC and CCSD board would collaborate to encourage DDCS.

Lee (2006, 81) wrote, "The Navajo worldview originates from the creation stories told to the people." He suggests that these stories connect Navajo people to the Diyin Dine'é (the Holy People) and that they help to shape Navajo cultural identity. According to Lee, the Navajo mold beliefs and values from the Navajo worldview "into a philosophy that benefits the individual's life" (2006, 81). For Navajo people to continue their cultural identity into the twenty-first century, Lee noted that the principles of K'é, Hózhǫ́, and Sa'ah Naaghái Bik'eh Hózhǫ́ǫn are vital and that they constitute the essence of Navajo life. Following Lee's imperative, Diné people should support and celebrate schools like DDCS that actively promote empowerment of youth using Diné language and teachings.

Manuelito (2006, 25) writes that Diné ancestors recognized leaders as having the following values: "*Hadine'e Baa Haajinizin* (having compassion for your people), *Hadine'e Ayoi'ojo'nih* (having love for your people), and *Hadine'e hwil Niliigo* (respecting your people)." She asserts that a "powerful Diné (Navajo) worldview persists in contemporary Diné (Navajo) society and continues to frame the world for its people and children who daily are conflicted by the demands of American schooling and the Euro-western worldview" (Manuelito 2006, 9). The GC always emphasized that their students should be proud to be Diné and that they should learn about their unique Diné history and culture, alongside learning English academics.

STUDENT PERFORMANCE ON STATE ASSESSMENTS

The NMPED (2016) *Tribal Education Status Report School Year 2015–16* for New Mexico public schools indicates an average 27 percent proficiency in reading and average 10 percent proficiency in math by the state's Native American students (http://nmindianeducact.org/wp-content/uploads/2017/10/Tribal-Education-Status-Report-Nov-2016.pdf). In fact, "low academic achievement and low graduation rates among Native American students constitute a pattern that has persisted for decades, not only in New Mexico but also nationally" (Deschenie 2013, 7). Although DDCS had existed for only two and a half years when its third grade took the PARCC test, its students' performance was expected to be on par with state expectations and with the performance of local district schools, such as CCSD, which had been in existence for close to half a century. There was no consideration of what DDCS had endured due to its great start-up challenges. There were great inequities of resources and stability between the brand-new charter school and existing school districts, but none of that was factored into the metrics that branded the school with an F two years in a row.

Larry Emerson, a Diné community activist and scholar from Tsé Daak'aan, New Mexico, identified common failures of the public school system as follows:

- A failure to work with the principles and politics of tribal sovereignty and self-determination in education.
- A failure to engage Indigenous-Western and traditional-modern dichotomies and frameworks as they relate to pedagogy, ideology, power, epistemology, research, race, gender, culture, language, history, identity, and philosophy.

- A failure to engage race, racialization, and racism issues in schools.
- The assumption that state law trumps tribal law, culture, language, history, and politics, thereby subordinating tribal communities. (Deschenie 2013, 24)

Emerson long advocated for Indigenous community critique of the public school system and strongly supported DDCS. Lomawaima and McCarty (2006, 170) wrote that such critique could help to recognize the danger "in attempts to standardize and homogenize the linguistically and culturally diverse peoples who comprise the nation's citizenry."

Even with national, state, and Diné legislation and policy in place to support it, providing language and culture education in schools is a challenge. The National Indian Education Association website lists critical national Indian Education laws. The New Mexico Indian Education Act (NMIEA) requires government-to-government consultation and emphasizes the importance of tribal language, history, and government curricula and of conducting "indigenous research and evaluation for effective curricula for tribal students" (NMIEA § 22–23A-1–8: NMSA 1978, 2007, para E5).

School boards and school administrations can support language and culture instruction under the existing laws and policies. However, they respond disparately. Deloria wrote, "Wherever possible local communities should begin to take control of primary and part of secondary education . . . [and] emphasize control over curriculum, with teaching about tribal history, tribal customs and traditions, and tribal language at the earliest possible age with maximum use of traditional people" (Deloria and Wildcat 2001, 157–58). However, there has always been resistance by the school board and school leadership to the permanent empowerment of the local Native community. In New Mexico, only one Native community, Zuni Pueblo, forced the creation of its own school district in 1980, asserting local control over the education of their children.

Many public schools were first opened on land adjoining the Navajo Reservation to serve non-Native communities and only later were expanded to serve the Native communities. For example, the CCSD was formed in the mid-twentieth century by combining off-reservation schools and schools on the Navajo Reservation: "In 1953 all schools in the valley region west of Farmington were consolidated to create an independent district, and to include Shiprock and Toadlena on the reservation"

(Patten 1959, 25). Today over half of the CCSD schools are located on the Navajo Reservation. From the outset of consolidation, there has been friction between the non-Native community and the Navajo communities over how the district operates.

Power struggles like this have long been common to the New Mexico public school districts that encompass the Navajo Reservation. Manuelito (2006) wrote about hostility and resentment between the Navajo community and the Mormon community in Ramah when the Navajo community began developing its own school. She quotes Rosemary Blanchard, a non-Native researcher, who said, "They [Anglo Mormons] were unhappy about not being given a role in school affairs" (Manuelito 2006, 11). Such struggles naturally impact the power dynamics among school boards, district administrations, and the Diné communities.

RESILIENCE AGAINST THE ODDS

DDCS opened as a state-authorized elementary dual language charter school in fall 2014 under a five-year charter contract. It is the first New Mexico public elementary charter school to serve the Navajo Nation. The school was reauthorized as a CCSD district charter school beginning with the 2019–20 academic year. In fall 2018, when the school sought a charter renewal with CCSD, the district initially approved a one-year charter with conditions. The school faced an uphill battle to meet those conditions, regarding academic performance, facility and site conditions, land lease, and school finance. Nonetheless, in spring 2019, after appealing to the New Mexico Public Education Department (NMPED), the school was granted a second five-year district charter contract. Keeping DDCS a reality was a continuous struggle in the first five years.

The school faced many challenges. Facilities and land were issues. In the first year, the school was housed in an empty Navajo Nation Head Start facility six miles from Shiprock; it was later relocated to five portable buildings adjacent to the Shiprock Chapter. The small parcel of land did not allow space for sports or extensive PE, and there was no expanded facility capacity. With no kitchen, the school purchased meals from CCSD. The status of the land on which the school was located was questionable; due to the lack of a long-term lease, temporary conditional leases were used. The Navajo Nation and the chapter both control aspects of land leasing.

In the first two years, the school had promising enrollment, but thereafter the numbers fluctuated. According to families, the lack of bus transportation was a huge factor. It became a deal breaker for some when a vehicle broke down or when parents had work schedule changes. Attendance was negatively impacted, and lower enrollment impacted funding.

School leadership is critical for a brand-new school, but there was unavoidable administrative turnover. The first administrator, who was also the elementary bilingual teacher, left after year one. In the second year, a contracted licensed principal came on site periodically. For the first two years, there was also a full-time operations director who arranged for purchase of buildings, for development of infrastructure, and for transition between two sites. In the third through fifth years, there was one licensed full-time administrator to oversee all administration and operations. Staff had to learn almost from scratch with each transition. School budget constraints limited hiring to adequately develop and manage the school. Administrators had to multitask among a constantly increasing number of duties and deadlines.

Teacher turnover was also problematic. It became increasingly challenging to find teachers with both elementary and bilingual licensure, essential in a dual language school. Most bilingual licensed teachers had only taught Navajo and not English academic content. The Department of Diné Education provides the Native American Language and Culture Certificate, which NMPED will accept, but the recipients are not always ready for planning and teaching all of the content they become certified in. And the school could not receive bilingual education funding if teachers did not have appropriate credentials, including for ESL instruction. In general, the availability of bilingual licensed or qualified Native language certified staff is decreasing annually, which is a paramount threat to the future of Navajo language instruction.

STATE REVIEW AND ACCOUNTABILITY SYSTEM

NMPED and the New Mexico Public Education Commission, the chartering authority, through a Performance Review and Accountability

System, enforce the purpose of New Mexico Charter Schools Act. Academic performance and fiscal and organizational accountability are measured through data submissions, annual school visits, and an annual performance review. Student academic achievement, in addition to compliance with applicable laws, rules, policies, and the charter contract, are all considered for a school's annual ratings.

In the initial four years of DDCS's operations, NMPED issued annual school report cards. In the first year, only K–1 grades were served (thereafter, a grade was added annually). Since no standards-based assessments were required in year one, the school earned a B on its report card. In the next three years, the school earned two Fs and a D. Every year brought an onslaught of requirements and corrective actions to meet: student assessment performance, teaching staff credentials, instructional hour timelines, response to intervention, attendance, reporting, and so on. In the third year, when the third grade had to take the state-mandated PARCC test, the teacher felt pressured to prepare the students with extensive practice, as did all of the teachers thereafter. Large chunks of instructional time were relegated to test prep. One reading grant required the school to block out 90–120 minutes for English literacy, leaving limited time for math, Diné language/culture, PE, meals, or recess. Students showed uneven proficiency, even with the literacy time block, response to intervention, and skill drills in place. The state teacher evaluation system was tied to student performance, which weighed on the teachers.

The families, some of whom had experienced negative pressure around academic achievement in other schools, became disillusioned when DDCS increasingly emphasized academic achievement and skills development. Some questioned why the school was testing like the other schools, thinking perhaps a charter school would be exempt. Others had difficult stories about how their children had been neglected in other schools, leaving them behind in certain academic skills. Even so, some students exhibited incredible positive change in their behavior after only a few months at DDCS. Still, it took time to engage the students more positively in their learning, and the rigid state school evaluation process did not recognize their emotional growth. The primary focus was meeting the academic goals tied to annual testing. If not met, these became part of the school's corrective action.

CONCLUSION

"Kill the Indian, and save the man"—that was the stated aim of Carlisle Indian Industrial School founder Richard H. Pratt in 1892, and it would become perhaps the most infamous goal of education for Indian people. Over a century has passed since this pronouncement, yet the hegemonic school systems serving Diné students have done little to prevent the ongoing demise of Diné language and identity. The State Performance Review and Accountability System in place during DDCS's first charter contract, from 2014 to 2019, did not address Diné language and identity. Though the school's students excelled on the Oral Diné Language Assessment from 2016 to 2018, their accomplishment was ignored in the state report cards. Rather, corrective action plans had to be written regarding the school's reading and math goals. Nevertheless, the goals of teaching Diné language and culture remain part of the school's renewed charter.

A report commissioned by NMPED states, "Culturally responsive education requires systemic reform and transformation in educational ideologies. Such a task is not easily accomplished in a rigid public school structure that is bound by state and federal laws" (Jojola 2010). True reform of the state's public schools is not likely to happen if Diné people must engage in litigation to sustain one small school like DDCS. There will be little accountability for school districts to provide an education that addresses Diné self-identity unless Diné community members themselves assert the enduring value of Diné stories and ways. For these changes to happen, significant research by Indigenous scholars that calls for an Indigenous lens and for the implementation of Indigenous-based education, currently known to a small minority of educators, must become essential professional development or education for community members, administrators, and tribal leaders alike. For the Diné charter schools, the Navajo Nation should seek to become a state charter school authorizer.

As we learn from the Diné story of the wolf, bluebird, hummingbird, and mountain lion, there is a real need for the collaboration of a variety of leaders and for a range of skills that will help us survive as a people. The challenge is for the Diné people to purposefully recall and apply these teachings to the education of Diné children. Diné identity and Diné survival are at stake.

The moccasin-making activity described at the beginning of this chapter took place in a summer enrichment program. It could happen only outside of the regular academic year due to the daily four to five hours needed to properly allow the families involved to undertake the rigorous learning involved. Moccasin makers are hard to find. The needed materials are expensive. The instruction is intensive and requires extended time. In the five years the school existed, this was the first time the students had access to this rare and exceptional learning opportunity. The sewn moccasins would be the first moccasins made and owned by the students. Nothing will make those who made their own moccasins prouder than to be able to wear them as Diné people are meant to.

REFERENCES CITED

Ah Nee-Benham, M. K. P., and E. T. Cooper. 2000. "Gathering Together to Travel to the Source: A Vision for a Language and Culture-Based Education Model." In *Indigenous Educational Models for Contemporary Practice: In Our Mother's Voice*, edited by M. K. P. Ah Nee-Benham and E. T. Cooper, 1–23. Mahwah, NJ: Lawrence Erlbaum Associates.

Deloria, V., Jr., and D. R. Wildcat. 2001. *Power and Place: Indian Education in America*. Golden, CO: Fulcrum Resources.

Deschenie, Quintina V. 2013. "K'é Bee: Diné Community Leadership, an Emergence Story." PhD diss., New Mexico State University, Las Cruces.

Jojola, Theodore (proj. coord.). 2010. *Indian Education in New Mexico, 2025*. Study contracted by New Mexico Public Education Department, Indian Education Division and conducted by Eight Northern Indian Pueblos Council Inc. and Indigenous Education Study Group. https://turtletalk.files.wordpress.com/2011/05/nmindianedrpt2011apr24111.pdf.

Lee, L. L. 2006. "Navajo Cultural Identity: What Can the Navajo Nation Bring to the American Indian Identity Discussion Table?" *Wicazo Sa Review* 21 (2): 79–103.

Lomawaima, K.T., and T. L. McCarty. 2006. *"To Remain an Indian": Lessons in Democracy from a Century of Native American Education*. New York: Teachers College Press.

Manuelito, K. D. 2006. "A Diné Perspective on Self-Determination: An Exposition of an Egalitarian Place." *Taboo: The Journal of Culture and Education* 10 (1): 7–27.

New Mexico Public Education Department (NMPED). 2016. *Tribal Education Status Report School Year 2015–16*. Santa Fe: New Mexico Public Education Department.

Patten, C. T. 1959. "The Farmington Story." *Farmington (New Mexico) Daily Times*, April 30, 1959.

CHAPTER 10

RETHINKING SCHOOL DISCIPLINE FOR NATIVE STUDENTS, EDUCATORS, AND ADMINISTRATORS

MICHAEL "MIKKI" CARROLL

Part of what is really important, is to be able to have empathy for people, to understand the pain of another person, even if you haven't experienced what they have.

LUCI TAPAHONSO, "THE MOON IS SO FAR AWAY: AN INTERVIEW WITH LUCI TAPAHONSO" BY ANDREA M. PENNER

Yá'át'ééh shik'éí dóó shidine'é, Shí éí Michael Carroll yinishyé, Dziłahnii nishłį, Hooghantání bashishchiin, Tódích'íí'nii dashicheii, Kinłichíí'nii dashinalí, Ákót'éego diné asdzáán nishłį.

K'É (CLAN RELATIONS–DINÉ INTRODUCTION)

MY COLONIZED name is Michael "Mikki" Carroll, and I was born in Shiprock, New Mexico, but grew up in Durango, Colorado, and Farmington, New Mexico. I am the oldest of four siblings, two sisters and two brothers. My mother's side of the family originates from Chinle, Arizona, and Naschitti, New Mexico, and my father's side from Shiprock and Hogback, New Mexico. Our last name "Carroll" derives from Hwééldi, the Navajo Long Walk of 1864, a dark time in Diné history when our Diné people were forced from their ancestral homelands to march to the Bosque Redondo encampment at Fort Sumner, New Mexico, led by Kit Carson. According to my great-grandmother, an Irish soldier with the last name "O'Carroll" led my ancestors from Canyon de Chelly in Chinle, Arizona, to the encampment at Fort Sumner. The Irishman was part of Kit Carson's regiment, soldiers who could not pronounce Diné names so groups were formed and identified by the soldiers' last names. Our family continued to carry the colonized name "Carroll" from generation to generation as a symbol of the resistance and perseverance of our Diné people. However, this does not define my family and relatives—it demonstrates our strength, courage, and resilience.

MY STORY

I have two beautiful boys, one a grown adult and out of the house on his own and one younger son in his middle school years. I am currently a doctoral student at the University of New Mexico in an all-Indigenous cohort, the Native American Leadership in Education program in the College of Education. In my current position, I am the head of school for high school in an Albuquerque public charter school, the Native American Community Academy (NACA), where I have worked since its inception in 2006. I started as a student teacher, then progressed to middle school teacher, dean of students, and now head of school for high school. Throughout my fourteen years at NACA, I have worked with students and parents in various capacities as a teacher, advisor, coach, facilitator, disciplinarian, and administrator. My educational roles have included curriculum developer, content facilitator, cross country coach, advisory liaison, advocate for students and families, disciplinarian, policy analyst, and school administrator. However, my areas of greatest interest are school discipline policies and practices, zero tolerance, and restorative justice. I am interested in these particular topics because many students often get caught in a system that pushes them out and labels them as problem students. Part of my interest stems from a family member who was caught in the school-to-prison pipeline, a disturbing national trend wherein students are funneled from public school into the criminal system, a process of criminalizing youth that is carried out by disciplinary policies and practices within schools that put students into contact with law enforcement.

I strongly believe educational environments are challenged with balancing academics and school discipline, in essence the school's balance and harmony, *hózhǫ́*, of any school. This topic often lacks discussion in schools due to its negative reflections on students, staff, administrators, or a school's image. Yet if addressed properly, these discussions can reduce disruptions, create positive environments, and ensure proactive measures to promote healthy relationships in the school setting that promote cultural identity. Administrators and educators cannot discuss academic achievement data without discussing school discipline data to reflect a *whole* school; highlighting only successful students diminishes suspended or expelled students, further pushing them out of public school systems. Schools cannot address low performance and achievement gaps if disciplinary practices are not discussed; discipline disparity exists. Schools have the ability to redefine school discipline and have dialogue with the community about behavior expectations while moving away from punitive models like zero tolerance. Zero tolerance refers to school discipline policies and practices that mandate predetermined consequences, typically severe, punitive, and exclusionary (e.g., out of school suspension and expulsion), in response to specific types of student misbehavior—regardless of the context or rationale for the behavior. Reviewing school data or climate surveys will show trends regarding relationships between students and teachers: teachers who need support with classroom behavior management plans or repeat offenders who need support. School leaders who work in Indigenous communities can consider discipline models that align with community values or tribal values to support healthy identities and relationships with students. In this chapter, I will discuss the challenges of school discipline among teachers and administrators from my own personal experiences with the hope that educators and administrators will rethink and encourage positive school discipline models, as well as consider how self-determination and sovereignty play a role in redefining school discipline in classrooms and schools to address outdated punitive colonized methods that continue to regenerate trauma for our Diné students as well as other Native students in our schools today.

Growing up in a strict Diné family, we were expected to act and behave in accordance with Diné values and philosophies to include balance and harmony of life, hózhǫ́, clans and kinship, respecting elders, respecting our parents, respecting Mother Earth, and the natural processes, seasons, and animals that make up the integral parts of the universe. We were taught to get up early with the sun and pray with *tádídíín* (corn pollen), symbolizing harmony, to ground our being with nature through prayer and ceremonies, which has taught me the responsibilities of honoring hózhǫ́, a balance in my life, as well as my relations, *k'é* with family and friends. As the oldest child in my family, I grew up with many responsibilities in my home, including helping to raise and take care of my siblings, serving as another parent figure. At times, I had to be the disciplinarian when my parents were busy at work and kept order in the house to ensure household chores and duties were maintained. During summer months we were sent to my great-grandmother's home in Chinle on the Navajo Reservation to help herd sheep, chop wood, carry water, clean the hogan, or cook. And if we complained or wanted to be lazy, my great-grandmother, who spoke no English, would lecture us in Navajo about the importance of work ethic, reminding us that our ancestors struggled to ensure we thrived and expected our people to carry on traditions, language, and heritage to maintain our existence in the colonized world. Kids today are not taught about their identity and the struggle of our people; that is why they are lost and do not understand the resiliency of our Diné people who survived the Long Walk. Our people were challenged, forced at gunpoint to walk to Bosque Redondo, forced to assimilate into a colonial life at Fort Sumner; women were raped, our Diné people were abused, and they suffered until Diné leaders were able to negotiate their release and they were allowed to return to our ancestral homelands. Part of the negotiation included education for our people because they knew we would live in the colonized world, which was proven, as upon arriving home from Fort Sumner, our people were assimilated into a colonial lifestyle, having to adapt to government changes imposed on them and relocating off reservation lands, our youth forced into a punitive school system that saw no value in our traditions and heritage.

As my great-grandmother shared stories of growing up, she would lose her thoughts in reflection of the past and would speak strongly about our future, reminding me and my siblings that we had to work hard in life. She said, "Kids today do not know hard work, ethics, and discipline; they have never experienced the Long Walk." The challenge is in Navajo we do not have a word for "try"; either you do the work or you don't do the work. My great-grandmother passed away when I was twelve, and her message would resonate for years to come among me and my siblings, which left an impression in our hearts and minds through adulthood. After reflecting years later, her strong words would regenerate themselves in the pain and grief she experienced during the boarding school era during which Native children were stripped of their identities to eradicate Native culture and languages. The harsh physical abuse and punitive punishments she spoke of when she spoke her language left scars from that era of schooling. Colonial discipline practices from that era would continue to manifest in our schools for years to come. School discipline has always been a challenge for educators, and zero tolerance laws started shaping our perceptions of misbehavior, leading to a mindset of criminalizing minor behavior issues as a way to control students. An easy answer to removing "problem students" is to suspend them, which is a colonial idea and practice. Trying to make students obedient and complacent with authority or to control behavior and actions through zero tolerance punishments are not the answers. Our students who are subjugated to this type of school discipline practice will only end up in a school-to-prison pipeline with no future if we do not change how we think about behavior in schools. What is the motivation or the under-pinnings of this behavior? How can educators change their response to misbehavior in the classroom? Does school discipline policy help students or increase the behavior? Does school discipline policy align with cultural norms or behavior?

As I think back during the time I spent with my great-grandmother, I reflect on her teachings and I question how much this impacted my parenting skills with my own boys and how many other families suffered abuse and trauma that was repeated through discipline approaches, generation after generation. When do we recognize this trauma and change it for our families, our classrooms, and our communities? I consider myself a strict parent, yet I want my boys to understand accountability for decisions they make while maintaining healthy relations and communication to keep their cultural identity intact. Part of understanding how I apply discipline was through reflections with my own children. What is the balance? In the classroom, I worked with my students observing, listening, and participating in communication to get to the root of student misbehaviors. My students shared with me that one of the reasons they misbehaved was that the adults in their lives did not take time to listen to them, and the only way they were able to get attention was through misbehaving. As a teacher, I was able to read students, have conversations with them, hear them, listen to them, and promote their voices to support accountability and consequences of their actions. When I took time to listen to my students, they misbehaved less, and I never sent a student out of my classroom. Rather, we had talking circles (a restorative method) about how their behaviors affected learning in my class. This method gave them a platform to share and understand accountability—a teachable moment rather than a punitive response. I wanted to maintain my working relationship with my students.

From the teacher's perspective, your goal is to continually grow your craft. Great teachers often reflect on their practice, whether that is developing lessons, teaching, or reviewing behavior management plans. Teachers want to maximize their time in the classroom. Teachers are willing to try new approaches for teaching and reaching students at all levels. But when a lesson goes awry, teachers take note. What happened? Did I or the student have an off day? Is someone frustrated? Was my lesson challenging? Were students engaged? Was my classroom management plan effective? Why or why not? Teachers reflect through self-talk often on their drive home after work, pondering what happened in class that day. Although tempers can escalate on both sides at times, adults should not lose control; they should use strategies to de-escalate the situation. Honestly, the root of any behavior can be worked out together, with patience. As a teacher my goal was to keep all students in class no matter the issue unless there were serious incidents, which were rare. Recognizing the value of the relationship between teachers and students, I worked at two key actions, "hearing" and "listening" to my students: hearing, an opportunity to state one's case, versus listening, giving one's attention to be ready to respond. This allowed me to establish a student's voice in my classroom while maintaining accountability, upholding my expectations, and remaining consistent while building rapport with students. Part of my experience as a teacher and maintaining my classroom management came from my Diné upbringing and understanding that k'é (relations) are crucial and that we are all related in some capacity and how we treat each other has implications for hózhǫ́ (balance and harmony).

As an administrator I learned that without effective discipline policies, school administrators can be prone to violating student and parent rights. Authority should not be about control; parents should be able to come to administrators without pre-judgment or feeling intimidated. School leaders should ensure school staff and teachers are effectively trained with de-escalation strategies, communication, cross-cultural understanding, and an understanding of compilation laws for school discipline policies as well as special education laws in their school. This can make the difference in understanding and knowing your rights as a teacher or administrator to protect your credentials as well as your school's. Liabilities can make or break a school, so it is important staff know the discipline compilation laws in their state. School discipline policies can align to cultural norms of the community and support healthier ways to deal with school discipline for their students. For example, rather than suspend a male repeat offender in school, I might gather a council of male teachers, leaders, fathers, and uncles to work with the student to discuss the offense and how it pertains to his cultural identity and role in the community. What does it mean to uphold the cultural values from a male perspective? What behaviors need to change? How can this support his cultural identity in the future? My hope is that promoting healthy accountability means students will work harder to uphold these values in the community. If I only consider punitive discipline practices, I take the key element of a learned lesson away from students because a decision is made for them, so there is no accountability.

Today, Diné teaching and values are being challenged with fewer and fewer Diné language speakers and cultural knowledge holders; some Diné students reject their Diné identity to fit into mainstream society and ideology, and they would rather embrace other cultural identities. Family structures have also changed, with more families moving from rural areas and into urban areas, creating disconnections from the Diné community either unintentionally or intentionally. Other contributing factors noted are impacts from alcohol, drugs, suicide, poverty, and other financial concerns that have heightened stress and relationships in the home, with children who are often caught in a crossfire resulting in verbal or physical abuse. Students look to school as a safe environment to be among friends and adults who care about their well-being; however, when the environment is no longer safe or the adults in the environment compromise the relationships, misbehavior increases and trust is lost.

Discipline rates in schools nationwide are at an all-time high, especially among students of color. Although Native students make up smaller student proportions in statewide statistics, discipline rates are disproportionate among both male and female Native students. Exclusionary discipline numbers for both in-school and out-of-school discipline, including expulsions, among male and female Native students are also high. Many questions arise as discipline concerns escalate in public, charter, and Bureau of Indian Affairs schools for many Diné families who are grappling with how to handle discipline situations when administrators do not follow their own policies or support teachers who have violated student or parent rights. For example, incidents like when a non-Native public school teacher cuts a Diné student's hair in class as a joke while using racial slurs or making racial comments about cultural ceremonies that non-Native teachers don't understand. Parents immediately are frustrated, angered, or discouraged about continuing to send their students back to these types of school environments and question whether school discipline practices are racially charged as continued colonial punitive practices go unpunished by administrators. Do staff, teachers, and administrators participate in culturally sensitive training? What are the relationships between students and teachers? How are administrators making discipline decisions? Oftentimes parents do not fully understand a school's discipline policy and how administrative decisions are made, especially when this includes law enforcement.

Punitive school discipline policies are being questioned and challenged as parents and communities are becoming more and more concerned. Students are being suspended and pushed out of school for minor infractions that could otherwise be handled internally or with parents through alternative methods. Consequences are not being given to students with input from students or parents but instead from zero tolerance perspectives due to colonial methods and thinking. Meanwhile, students do not learn accountability or responsibility, nor is learning happening from their negative decisions. Rather, schools are making discipline decisions for students and then sending them home to return to school after a few days out, creating a revolving door for students. Meanwhile, families are fighting an educational and juvenile justice system with little to no support because they are unfamiliar with school discipline policies and discipline laws. One such incident took place in my family.

My cousin Kee's (pseudonym) story is a prime example of how he became a victim of the school-to-prison pipeline. Kee was a special needs, seventh-grade student, rambunctious and full of wonder about the world and his place in it. Like many young males, he was self-conscious as he was starting puberty as well as trying to find his voice among peers. However, teasing and bullying for seventh-grade boys is common as they experience transitions and learn about relationships, which is often a time when teachers have their hands full with behavior and discipline concerns.

One day during class, another male student started teasing and bullying Kee. The other student grabbed Kee's pencil and ran off, laughing and teasing him. Kee demanded he give it back and sought the teacher's help to recover it. The teacher dismissed the behavior as boys being boys, which quickly escalated between the students. The student continued to tease Kee, running behind desks and avoiding Kee as he chased him. The teacher sat behind her desk engaged in other activities and did not respond to the commotion. Kee once again asked for help, but she ignored his requests to intervene. Eventually, the teacher looked up and noticed the two boys grabbing at each other. Kee demanded his pencil back, and the other student laughed at him. The boys ended up at the teacher's desk on each side of her continuing to try to get the pencil. The conflict escalated into an altercation between them when the teacher tried to intervene. Kee accidentally punched the teacher on her shoulder when he was aiming for the other student. The teacher finally addressed the behavior and took the boys to the office. All the while Kee knew his action got him in trouble, and he apologized to the teacher for his actions. The teacher, upset that she was hit, told the principal she was going to file assault charges against Kee.

The principal had no choice but to contact the police. Clearly, this non-Native teacher did not have any effective classroom management plans nor was she held accountable for her role in the situation. Yet she was allowed to file charges against Kee, causing Kee to get caught up in the school-to-prison pipeline. The police showed up at the school, arrested Kee, and took him to the juvenile detention center until his parents picked him up. The story would not be a happy one. He was caught in the juvenile justice system, which created a strain on his relationship with his father that ultimately led to their estrangement.

During his time in the detention center, he turned to other boys who were caught in the system and found solace with them, eventually bonding and joining their gangs while serving out his time. He became susceptible to gangs who became his family, further pushing him in another direction to fight to survive and find a niche in a juvenile system he should never have been a part of. As time passed, he only strengthened his bond with the gang brotherhood, which influenced his actions inside and outside of detention center, grooming him for another lifestyle in prison.

Kee's story is an example of how misguided school discipline can alter a student's life, using exclusionary discipline practices rather than finding opportunities to teach accountability in ways that are healthy, not punitive. Kee did not intend to hurt anyone. In fact, he had reached out for teacher support to address a behavioral concern. But the teacher's lack of response to his situation only contributed to the bullying antics he was dealing with. Why didn't the teacher address it immediately? Why did she wait? If she had taken control of the situation and de-escalated it, Kee would not have moved to strike another student out of frustration, and his life today would be different.

Teachers and administrators who work in schools or for our tribes need to understand that in order to instill positive healthy habits, as adults they should "hear" and "listen" to their students. Part of this response is to understand what I refer to as *cultural accountability*, which simply refers to school staff being accountable to the culture of the environment of the community they serve. What are the communal values that our students come to our school with? Does understanding a student's background, especially when a teacher is not familiar with the culture, matter to teachers? Why do Indigenous communities continue to allow colonial, punitive actions and beliefs to victimize our youth?

RELATIONAL IMPACT

Discipline can be a hot topic for schools as teachers and administrators are contending with socioemotional trauma among Native students and families on and off the reservation. Part of the trauma impacting families is largely due to socioemotional concerns regarding alcohol, drugs, suicide, physical abuse, and poverty. The impact can be seen in the behavior students exhibit in the classroom and on the playground, or between peers and teachers. Additionally, how school staff, teachers, and administrators respond to student misbehavior can also contribute to student outcomes. How adults treat one another in the work environment can also impact student behavior and school climate as students see them as role models. Is staff displaying healthy communication and interactions that are respectful? Students are watching and listening.

School climate surveys can be a way to support schools in gaining an understanding of the working relationships on campus. Administrators can promote positive healthy relationships while working with teachers and parents as well as supporting teachers in developing classroom management plans that reflect students' cultural backgrounds to promote buy-in. Schools that conduct school climate surveys with students, staff, parents, or the community gain feedback on best practices that support cultural knowledge and align with tribal community values. Schools that can advocate for discipline methods that promote cultural identity with *healthy* accountability will have opportunities to support a student's well-being and nurture an understanding of decisions and consequences through a cultural lens.

One of the advantages of tribally controlled schools is the opportunity to move toward self-determined methods that fully align with tribal knowledge systems. What does self-determination mean? Self-determination is the combination of attitudes and abilities for people to set goals for themselves while taking initiatives to meet those goals based on their needs. For schools with this autonomy, they can build discipline protocols and policies that support and foster tribal identity in ways that can decolonize disciplinary approaches for Diné and other Native students. Studies have shown that zero tolerance methods do not work; rather, they promote repeated negative behavior and even criminalize it, force students out of school, do not teach accountability, and institute colonial punishments and laws in ways that promote failure and dropping out of school. We have to do better for our Native students; they cannot share the same experiences of their grandparents. The cycle stops with us; Native educators and administrators can reform policies, decolonize punitive discipline methods, change how discipline is taught in colleges and universities, and institute cultural discipline practices and protocols that align with our tribes or communities to ensure those cultural connections remain intact, hózhǫ́.

When I was initially approached to contribute to this book, I reflected on my personal experiences and what contribution would make a difference in education. I have worked for a charter school for most of my educational career and had the opportunity to institute culturally relevant pedagogies that support cultural identity for Native students that are key components in instituting self-determination and sovereignty. My personal experiences as a teacher and administrator have further pushed me to evaluate educational systems that interact with our Diné identity and what needs to change to promote k'é and hózhǫ́. I believe that academics and school discipline work collectively as a balance to inform school performance and growth. Students are part of the community, and they are the developing leaders, advocates, and voices representative of our tribal community. Our ancestors saw the benefit of education as well as the sacrifice to ensure our sovereignty in the colonized world. Self-determination is our tribal community's voice to organize cultural knowledge systems, thoughts, and epistemology in relation to our beliefs, traditions, and heritage. How can self-determination and sovereignty play a role in how we discipline our children as we prepare them to uphold Diné culture, beliefs, and values for our people? The answer lies in how we treat our students and prepare them for the future based on our tribal values and norms. Are we promoting outdated punitive methods or are we preparing our students to carry our Diné values and beliefs for the next generation? What stories will our students share with their grandchildren—the same stories of our grandparents?

When our Diné students are suspended or pushed out, we take away opportunities for understanding consequences of decisions. As the words of our ancestor in this proverb state, "You cannot see the future with tears in your eyes." This topic has been a concern for me as a teacher and as an administrator for some time because I know firsthand the impact punitive punishments have on Native students, and the stories do not change when Native students transfer from school to school. Stories of harsh treatments and practices remain the same. To understand increasing achievement gaps between Native students and mainstream society, discipline policies need to be reevaluated. Historically, cruel and harsh punishments during the boarding school era created a generation of abuse and trauma for our people, creating a cycle of learned punitive behavior that has been passed down generation to generation, resulting in harsh disciplinary measures among families and in schools and in some cases increasing physical and verbal abuse in our Native homes and communities. When will the cycle stop?

A HOLISTIC PERSPECTIVE

My great-grandmother's teachings helped me to understand the world around me from a holistic perspective. Every personal decision an individual makes has a consequence, whether good or bad; a life lesson is learned, and we are accountable for the decisions we make. In our Diné values and philosophy, decisions manifest in the way we lead our own lives, in everything we do, influencing the directions our journeys take us in and how we think or how we act. Traditionally, many Native communities applied disciplinary practices to their children that were culturally meaningful and supported physical, spiritual, emotional, and social growth as a communal society. Iiná is our journey as Diné people to find our path to a good life, the value of maintaining life that is centered on balance and harmony, hózhǫ́.

Earlier I shared my Diné upbringing, Ákót'éego diné asdzáán nishłį́į́, and how this shaped my worldview through my own culture and language and personal experience, rooting my Diné connections to my own identity as a Diné mother, student, educator, and administrator. Even when I lived away from the Navajo Reservation, my acknowledgment of my Diné identity was my connection to my ancestors that hold truths today. What they envisioned for our Diné people's survival in dominant society was the resilience to maintain Diné values and beliefs and finding the balance and harmony, hózhǫ́, within ourselves to promote healthy living with healthy relationships, with k'é in every environment we're a part of. It was my great-grandmother's storytelling and stories that grounded me in my Diné identity and protected my resiliency, along with her reminder that my ancestors struggled during the Long Walk and endured difficult hardships. Her pain and suffering during the boarding school era and my cousin Kee's personal story are both stark examples of harsh, punitive discipline practices and policies that continue to underpin educational systems and promote failure for Native students. My personal reflection as a disciplinarian through the lenses of a mother, teacher, and administrator have helped me to recognize the conflict school disciplinary practices have with k'é and hózhǫ́. Student misbehavior in school is triggered when students are not heard or seen in school spaces or home environments. This can be remedied by simply checking in with students and asking if they are OK, creating opportunities to hear from our students.

For educators and administrators, studies have shown Native students thrive in schools that value their culture and promote culturally relevant classrooms.

Culturally relevant pedagogies in classroom instruction have proven to bridge academic proficiency and academic growth over the last few decades. Success stories like the Rough Rock Demonstration School in Arizona were considered model educational systems that promoted culturally relevant teaching that supported Diné students, highlighting Diné culture, Diné language, and academics to meet student achievement, breaking the cycle of colonized educational systems that removed student identity from schools. The roots of our Diné identity are being challenged as educators and administrators grapple with how to revitalize our Diné language and heritage. Many of our students leave the reservation for a better life and often forget the stories that grounded their identity. In my work and experience in schools, students often desired to learn about themselves and their people; however, they have lost the connection to home. Yet when they connect with an adult at school as a role model, it helps them to understand that their identity has value. This relationship of connection is powerful; it supports the grounding of their roots, belonging, and family. Traditional stories are essential for life lessons, which I found to be true through my own experience. My great-grandmother's stories and teachings reinforced and encouraged respectful behaviors that support positive decision-making and pushed me to reflect on my own journey, which encouraged me to assess my own parenting skills with my boys, setting a precedent for how my teaching will be passed down to my grandchildren.

CONCLUSION

Reflecting on my journey as an educator, I had to think about what makes a school successful in terms of identity. What is the Hózhǫ́ in a school and how do we see it in students and staff to promote it? This journey taught me to see the beauty around our students, families, and staff. Misbehavior will happen as a result of broken relationships and trust. Healing is part of change and offers opportunities for repairing broken relationships. As an educator, you want to prepare students to the best of their ability and in the process build rapport with students and families as students will become the leaders for tomorrow. Our Diné ancestors believed in the people as they negotiated education as part of the Treaty of 1868, recognizing that we would survive as a people with sovereignty in a colonized world. We have to believe in our students. But what we forget at times is that self-determination is our voice; how we prepare our students is our choice to empower them and ensure their well-being so they will continue to be strong and resilient for our people. We need to take back how to apply school discipline and teach decision-making skills and promote healthy accountability that aligns with our tribal values to strengthen our Diné identity. As I come to a close in this chapter, I would like to leave you with some questions to ponder: How will you decolonize outdated punitive discipline practices in your schools? How will these changes support your education system to promote cultural identity? How will you find hózhǫ́ in your students, staff, and school?

CHAPTER 11

TEACHER EDUCATION THAT UNDERSTANDS ITS PLACE

MICHAEL THOMPSON

W HEN LARRY Emerson passed away in the late summer of 2017, I lost one of the best, most humane friends I ever had. He taught me more about the Navajo worldview, the power of the hogan, the essentiality of the four sacred mountains, and reverence for the natural world than anyone I have ever known. His friendship shaped my understanding of what effective teaching for Navajo students might look like. Larry believed that when a Diné person is born, he or she is outfitted by the Holy People with everything needed to have a beautiful, fulfilling, and meaningful life. I hope to honor his faith in the Indigenous worldview as much as possible in this chapter on my experiences in teacher preparation and the Navajo Nation Teacher Education Consortium (NNTEC).

The concerns I'd like to address in this chapter are as follows: the critical shortage of teachers regionally; the difficulty of recruiting, training, and retaining effective teachers for Navajo schools; what I consider one of the most profound underlying challenges in education—the widespread lack of basic literacy skills; and finally, an honest acknowledgment that most schools serving Navajo students generally lack quality teacher training in culturally responsive pedagogy.

As a proud member of the Mvskoke Nation, I have been involved in Native education since 1978, when I became a young humanities instructor at Haskell Indian Junior College. I moved permanently to New Mexico as a high school English teacher more than twenty years ago, having fallen in love with a traditional Diné woman, an educator herself. During the past five years, I was the coordinator of the Alternative Licensure Program (ALP) at San Juan College and its representative to the NNTEC, during which time I conducted hundreds of classroom observations in the Four Corners, almost all of them in Navajo-serving schools. These circumstances have shaped my understanding of issues in Navajo teacher education today.

A recent report by New Mexico State University confirmed a rapid decline in individuals completing the state's Educator Preparation Programs, noting "a 33% decrease from 2009–2010 to 2017–2018" (NMSU College of Education Southwest Outreach Academic Research (SOAR) Lab 2018, 14). If the traditional pipeline into any crucial profession were to shrink by a third in less than a decade, that would seem desperately ominous, I'd say.

Among the reasons why individuals hesitate to become teachers, there are two that I heard repeatedly over five years of interviews with potential ALP candidates: low salaries coupled with greater testing requirements, including more forceful linking of student performance to teacher evaluation. In fact, almost a third of New Mexico teachers report "testing related job insecurity," compared to 12 percent nationally (NMSU College of Education Southwest Outreach Academic Research (SOAR) Lab 2018, 3). This seems to have created a widespread public notion that teaching is just not worth it.

Complicating our growing state teacher shortage has been an increasing number of retirements. According to a 2016 legislative brief, "While national figures downplay the importance of retirement in teacher shortages . . . data from Albuquerque Public Schools (APS) indicate retirement may play a bigger role in teacher shortages in New Mexico. In the 2012–2013 school year, teacher retirements made up nearly 40 percent of total departures" (New Mexico Education Retirement Board 2016, para. 3). This should be especially concerning, as the national figures are between 15 and 30 percent, according to various sources; apparently, there is no national dataset for annual data on teacher retirements (Aldeman 2015).

Two more challenges to teacher recruitment in the Southwest are the number of schools in remote locations and the number of students who are classified as English learners (ELs). More than a third of New Mexico schools are located in rural areas, and more than 70 percent of rural students are non-white, second in the nation after only Hawaii (Jimerson 2004, 5). Certainly, students on tribal lands are likely to live in remote communities and also to be classified as ELs. For many young people who dream of becoming teachers, the reality of living in isolation far from urban shopping and entertainment is simply a nonstarter, even if they are passionate about the profession.

Simultaneous with the decline in enrollments of traditional four-year degree programs has been a gradual increase in those for alternative licensure programs. San Juan College's ALP increased completers approximately 50 percent from 2014 to 2019, and similar increases have occurred in other state ALPs. It appears that alternative licensure offers an immediate path to employment for increasing numbers of degreed adults struggling to find work due to an unexpected relocation or who find their present work dissatisfying. For others who have long dreamed of teaching, it is an unexpected opportunity to take the shortest path ever into a classroom.

I would never argue that the ALP is the optimum form of teacher training, but certain factors determine whether it is effective or not. A major issue is the limited coursework. Designed for individuals who already possess a bachelor's degree, the instruction is, by nature, a kind of educational triage. The goal, frankly, is to train educated persons as quickly as possible in the basics of teaching because—ready or not—nearly all of them already are. This means the rudiments: how to manage behavior, how to write a lesson plan, how to assess learning, how to navigate standards and curricula. It doesn't leave much room for pedagogy in basic literacy or for critical concerns like culturally responsive pedagogy (CRP), for example. Yet, these are both essential matters for teaching Native learners.

State entrance requirements for ALPs have also been subject to change or left to institutional discretion. At least until 2019, it was up to the individual educator preparation program whether to require passage of basic skills tests for acceptance, and San Juan College maintains this requirement. As soon as someone is accepted into an ALP, he or she is immediately eligible for a two-year license. Without the ability to demonstrate competence themselves in reading, writing, and math, why would we expect beginning teachers to successfully develop those skills in their students?

That said, I have seen some excellent teachers survive this process; though the learning curve is incredibly steep, highly motivated individuals can emerge from their trial by fire as effective teachers. I think that an ALP works best when there is authentic mentoring and advising, the coursework is immediately practical and targeted, the face-to-face instruction is consistent and cohesive, and there is a high degree of cohort camaraderie.

While ALPs are increasingly available in online-only programs in order to reach more candidates, the value of face-to-face instruction and mentoring is simply too significant to abandon. According to San Juan College's completer surveys from 2014 to 2019, more than 85 percent of students preferred our hybrid model—a majority of work done online, paired with limited face-to-face classes (about fourteen hours per semester per course). Hands-on activities, lots of modeling, and ample opportunity for personal feedback and discussion are essential during a candidate's first challenging year.

It is very old news indeed that there exists a severe shortage of Native teachers in Native communities. When I taught in the Four Corners in the late 1990s, it was rare to see Navajo teachers in any significant numbers outside of Navajo language classes. Though this has slowly improved, the kind of representation we really need on the faculties of Navajo-serving schools is still a far-off vision. Fewer than 2 percent of the state's public school teachers are Native American in a state that has a Native population of 11 percent (Jennings 2020).

New Mexico in general has dismal academic indicators: rural National Assessment of Educational Progress (NAEP) scores are the lowest in the nation, the percent of rural students in poverty is the highest, and the graduation rate is second lowest in the nation (76.4 percent), exceeding only Alaska (Showalter et al. 2019, 124). Nationally, the poor academic performance of Native students has been well chronicled. Suffice it to say, Native students almost everywhere fall behind their non-Native peers: in New Mexico, 89 percent score below proficient in reading and 92 percent below proficient in math; their graduation rate is lowest of all groups at 66 percent (New Mexico Voices for Children 2019, 21–23).

In 2014, the *Albuquerque Journal* reported that 59 percent of all Native college freshmen in New Mexico needed remedial classes (Bush 2014, para. 8). But consider the scale of the challenge for the Navajo Nation. According to a 2019 Diné College press release, "an estimated 88 percent of students entering Diné College year-round must take remedial math, reading and English courses—and those classes are on average repeated at least twice" (https://www.dinecollege.edu/az-budget%20includes-1m -in-dine-college-remedial-education-pinto-scholarship-planned/).

Nevertheless, there are ongoing attempts at colleges everywhere to simply eliminate remedial education requirements (Mangan 2014), as if pretending that low placement scores are irrelevant will somehow magically enable these students to do college-level work. But sending weakly prepared high school graduates to college has consequences. When New Mexico's lottery scholarship suddenly surged college admissions decades ago, state senator John Arthur Smith noted, "(New Mexican colleges) enrolled a bunch of people that were not academically prepared for higher education yet and, as it turned out, the attrition rate was phenomenal" (Martinez 2020).

My work the last twenty years with Navajo students has profoundly impacted my understanding of the literacy crisis that has been building for more than half a century. I've engaged in many kinds of basic English instruction—from middle school to college-level developmental courses to high school workshops for the SAT and ACT and Accuplacer to coaching teacher candidates struggling to pass the National Evaluation Series skills tests. I've observed beginning teachers at every grade level struggling to teach the simplest rudiments of the English language, too often with instruction relying heavily on publisher and online resources that are woefully ineffective. Certainly, there are mountains of data to support such a characterization—the poor performance on national measures such as the NAEP, chronically low graduation rates, the high percentages of college freshmen placing into developmental coursework, and the alarming rate (27 percent) of would-be teachers in New Mexico who fail to pass the basic skills tests on their first try (NM Legislative Finance Committee 2018, 19).

The poor outcomes we have seen for decades are certainly not for lack of effort. Teachers are working harder than ever. Our entire P–16 system is trying desperately to teach language skills at every grade level, year after year, with little to show for it. Think about the implications. We devote hundreds, if not thousands, of hours every year of our students' lives to teaching and reteaching the basics of English—a language most (though not all) have been speaking since birth. And yet, at the end of all that, too many high school graduates and a disturbing number of our college graduates cannot demonstrate proficiency on the simplest tests of basic skills. How can we not conclude that there is something fundamentally wrong with the way we are teaching English? For me, this question is at the very heart of the 2019 Yazzie/Martinez ruling in New Mexico. If we sincerely want to improve literacy skills, we need to radically change the manner in which we teach English language arts (ELA), especially for second language learners.

Although the context of this chapter is not the appropriate place to go into great detail about how, specifically, ELA instruction must change, I will offer an outline of a system I believe makes more sense, especially for Navajo learners and second language and Native learners generally. More than anything, we need a simplified framework for teaching vocabulary, syntax, grammar, mechanics—one that provides a holistic understanding of English as a system and that is put into place in the very early grades, overlapping with the essential instruction in phonemic awareness and reading that must occur first. It is my belief that Indigenous learners generally work better from whole to part rather than part to whole, which unfortunately is the predominant way English is currently taught, and this belief aligns completely with Pewewardy's conclusions about field-dependence in Native learners (2002).

An Indigenous ELA framework could be built on the four basic functions of noun, verb, adjective, and adverb, rather than the myriad contradictory terminologies historically employed: participle, preposition, gerund, etc. This would allow us to teach word function through word structure, as students develop initial vocabulary knowledge, and then directly transfer that understanding to sentence structure, utilizing the same four categories but applied to sentence parts (including phrases and clauses) rather than to individual words. Many of our students' chronic errors result from their inability to understand these basic functions.

Of course, such a simple, comprehensive framework for ELA should be embedded in education preparation programs. Unfortunately, the English discipline as a whole began to ignore the teaching of such a framework decades ago, and we now have generations of teachers who themselves lack a comprehensive understanding of how English actually works. We need to correct that.

Let me turn to my final concern in Navajo education—the widespread absence of quality, culturally grounded instruction for Navajo students. This lack exists in public, tribal, and federal schools—both on and off the reservation. There are notable exceptions in places where highly motivated individual faculty and leadership treat Indigenous learning styles and integration of Navajo texts and other resources as a given. However, this commitment needs to be the standard everywhere Navajo students are served.

I must also note one often-overlooked obstacle to developing the kind of respectful educators that Native students need: the white privilege and institutional racism that exists in some of our colleges that train teachers. Although I was blessed with many colleagues at San Juan College who were strong allies for Native education and culture, I had my own personal encounters with white privilege, blatant enough to be deeply dismayed by it and to suspect it might exist in similar institutions. Although San Juan College has one of the largest bodies of Native students receiving AA degrees in the entire nation, the low degree of Native representation on the faculty and especially in the administration seems to represent a callousness toward Native concerns institution-wide that is deeply troubling. This is one of the many reasons I believe that the work of the Navajo Nation Teacher Education Consortium (NNTEC) could be so valuable.

For teachers to become truly culturally responsive to Navajo students is incredibly complex and time-consuming; to do it well requires, at the least, living and working within a Navajo community and doing a great deal of homework on the history and current concerns of the Navajo Nation. For many new teachers, that can seem like an impossible hill to climb. However, there are simple steps that all teacher training programs can take to improve upon the status quo. There is excellent scholarship by Stephanie A. Fryberg (Tulalip) and others on how Native students are negatively affected by the near total lack of accurate Native representation in curricula, texts, and other resources. However, addressing the basic step of integrating Navajo material into curricula is simply not that hard. Almost any motivated person can do it if he or she understands what it means and if one understands what kinds of resources can serve.

If you walked into a classroom and looked at the pictures on the wall, the books on the shelves, the posters and lists and motivational sayings that are common everywhere, would you know immediately if Navajo students were at home in that space? More significantly, if you looked at the curriculum being taught, would you see texts, activities, lessons, and examples in tasks and assignments that were reflective of Navajo life— especially contemporary life and the issues faced by the Navajo Nation and its citizens wherever they might live? I am not suggesting that all lessons and materials for core subjects should be built entirely from Navajo life, but certainly there should be regular and consistent representation.

When Common Core standards became the primary driver of pacing guides and lesson planning for K–12 education, one major shift required more attention to informational texts. Many teachers of Navajo students simply turned to whatever mainstream materials were provided by publishers and online programs to teach those skills, ignoring completely the perfectly useful Navajo newspaper that is published weekly and contains numerous fine informational articles, images, and editorial cartoons on complex subject matter directly related to the many immediate concerns of Navajo people.

The Navajo community also boasts an incredible number of immensely talented writers, especially poets, who deserve to be taught in literature classrooms everywhere, alongside Dickinson, Frost, Angelou, and Harjo. Why more of these Navajo writers are not regularly read in schools serving Navajo students mystifies me—not to mention the critical nonfiction by excellent scholars such as Jennifer Denetdale, Lloyd Lee, and many others. Happily, there is also a growing body of easily accessed writing on social media by and about Navajo society in all its facets. These texts could be adapted in endless ways for instruction of all kinds. And there are more Navajo and Native films and podcasts produced every day that could vivify Navajo classrooms everywhere.

I would like to briefly address one other significant concern that I hold for Navajo education looking into the future. Some people in public education have for years opposed the teaching of Native languages (including some Navajos). One of the most misguided but common arguments simply asserts that Navajo should be taught at home. While I am not myself bilingual or any kind of Native language expert, I do have strong feelings as a Native educator about this issue. Here are four big reasons these people are very wrong:

1. A majority of the grandparents and great-grandparents of present-day Navajo students lived through the boarding school era, many forbidden from speaking English. They raised their own children speaking English at home, not Navajo. Those children are today's parents, and many of them now lack the skills to successfully teach their own children fluent Navajo. National, state, and tribal laws recognize this and strongly support Native language instruction for Native students wherever possible.

2. No one says English should be taught only at home. Yet the vast majority of children entering first grade speak fluent English. Why then do we devote another twelve years to the study of English? Because language is incredibly important to master and because it is incredibly complex. Because language leads to literature and literature helps us to understand ourselves as individuals and as a people. The same is true of Navajo, and Navajo has the added burden of being threatened with extinction.

3. The imperative for teaching Native languages in our schools is much greater than simply providing bilingual education for bilingual speakers. If all schools in the United States stopped teaching French, Japanese, or Arabic tomorrow, those languages would continue to thrive in their linguistic motherlands. This is simply not so for Navajo or Apache or Lakota or any other Native languages. They are unique American languages, and if we do not fight to preserve them, very soon they will die.

4. With the death of each language, important aspects of these tribal cultures will also die. This cultural genocide has been the covert, if not the admitted, goal of many government policies dealing with Indians all along. Ask the opponents of language revitalization if they support the cultural genocide of Native people, and if the answer is no, ask them to explain how one saves a culture without also saving its language.

This brings me to the significance of the NNTEC, in existence since the 1990s. Under the current chairmanship of Henry Fowler, this committed group of culturally sensitive teacher educators, from an array of teacher prep institutions across the Southwest, has the potential to provide both vision and capacity to foster the kind of significant reform in teacher education that could fundamentally transform outcomes for schools across the Navajo Nation and in its sizeable border communities. Existing outside of the individual politics and privilege that can some-times create dysfunction in individual college programs, the consortium could develop common much-needed solutions to the challenges that face each institution separately when it comes to quality, culturally aware teacher preparation.

Consortium partners could collaborate on solving the basic skills needs of potential teacher candidates; they could serve as an effective clearing house for Navajo resources for culturally responsive lessons and instruction, such as the Math Circles materials developed by Fowler and others. Working with the Office of Navajo Nation Scholarship and Finan-cial Assistance and Department of Diné Education, they could involve a variety of Navajo scholars, educators, and artists in the development of initiatives that speak directly to the Navajo Nation's own educational standards.

The problems that exist in Navajo Nation education are large and complex. It is unlikely that individual teacher prep programs have either the will or the resources to solve them in isolation. The Navajo Nation Teacher Education Consortium may be our best hope of making the difference.

REFERENCES CITED

Aldeman, C. 2015. "How Many Teachers Retire Each Year?" *Teacher Pensions* (blog), June 19. https://www.teacherpensions.org/blog/how-many-teachers-retire-each-year.

Bush, M. 2014. "LFC Panel Calls Remedial Course Ineffective." *Albuquerque Journal*, March 21. https://www.abqjournal.com/372105/lfc-panel-calls-remedial-courses-ineffective-2.html.

Jennings, T. 2020. "2020 Legislative Session: Public Education Issues Will Dominate Session, with Focus on At-Risk Students." *New Mexico In Depth*, January 17. http://nmindepth.com/2020/01/17/public-education-issues-will-dominate-session-with-focus-on-at-risk-students/.

Jimerson, L. 2004. "Teachers and Teaching Conditions in Rural New Mexico." A Pub-lication of the Policy Program of the Rural School and Community Trust. https://www.ruraledu.org/user_uploads/file/teachers_newmexico.pdf.

Mangan, K. 2014. "Push to Reform Remedial Education Raises Difficult Questions for Colleges." *Chronicle of Higher Education*, April 8. https://www.chronicle.com/article/Push-to-Reform-Remedial/145817.

Martinez, A. 2020 "NM Legislature: What You Need to Know About Free College." *Daily Lobo*, January 21. https://www.dailylobo.com/article/2020/01/opportunity-scholarship-about-to-see-day-in-legislature.

New Mexico Education Retirement Board. 2016. "LESC Hearing Brief: Teacher and School Leader Retirement Trends." https://www.nmlegis.gov/handouts/ALESC%20081716%20Item%207%20RetirementTrends%20brief.pdf.

New Mexico Voices for Children. 2019. *2019 NM Kids Count Data Book: Tending Our Garden*. https://www.nmvoices.org/wp-content/uploads/2020/01/NMKidsCount-DataBook2019-web.pdf.

NM Legislative Finance Committee. 2018. "Teacher and School Leader Preparation Programs." Program Evaluation Unit Progress Report. https://www.nmlegis.gov/Entity/LFC/Documents/Program_Evaluation_Progress_Reports/LFC%20Progress%20Report%20-%20Educator%20Preparation%20Programs.pdf.

NMSU College of Education Southwest Outreach Academic Research (SOAR) Lab. 2018. "New Mexico Educator Vacancy Report." https://alliance.nmsu.edu/files/2018/10/2018-New-Mexico-Educator-Vacancy-Report.pdf.

Pewewardy, C. 2002. "Learning Styles of American Indian/Alaska Native Students." *Journal of American Indian Education* 41 (3): 22–56.

Showalter, D., S. L. Hartman, J. Johnson, and B. Klein. 2019. "Why Rural Matters 2018–2019: The Time Is Now." A Report by the Rural School and Community Trust and Our Partners: College Board and the School Superintendents Association (AASA). http://www.ruraledu.org/WhyRuralMatters.pdf.

CHAPTER 12

BRING IT TO US

A Message for Teacher Preparation University-District Partnerships

RICHARD FULTON

UNDERSTANDING AN Indigenous perspective is important when developing partnerships in Diné communities as local schools seek to integrate Diné culture and language into their curriculum. This perspective is particularly important when an outside entity, such as a college or university, partners with Native American–serving school districts to best serve the local communities. Relationships can be strengthened when college personnel and programs reach directly into the communities, engage with teacher candidates and local educators, and build long-lasting relationships with schools and districts. Strong relationships allow individuals in the programs to customize recruitment and work together when grant funded programs seek external partnership. It is especially important when many school districts across the Navajo Nation are experiencing teacher and educator shortages.

Fort Lewis College began reaching out to regional partners in the early 1990s with efforts to respond to Navajo Nation president Peterson Zah's call for the creation of five hundred new Navajo teachers in five years. Under a 1992 Ford Foundation grant, faculty members Gary Knight and Linda Simmons and Native American Center director Farrin Webb met with many members of the Central Consolidated School District and Farmington School District to establish what is now known as the

Fort Lewis College Teacher Outreach Program. The Fort Lewis College Teacher Outreach Program offered teacher aides with associate's degrees and at least sixty credits an avenue to earn a bachelor of arts in bicultural studies and coursework leading to New Mexico elementary education K–6 teaching certification. More than twenty-five years later, nearly three hundred Navajo teacher aides, community members, and teachers have earned their New Mexico teaching license and/or their TESOL (Teaching English to Speakers of Other Languages) certificate.

What can be learned from these efforts and how has it has been sustained over the years using an Indigenous perspective?

FAMILY COMES FIRST

In Diné communities, family commitments are paramount. Family commitments include helping with household and ranch duties, childcare, participating in ceremonies and celebrations, and pursuing continuous education to inspire individuals to achieve more education than their parents. Household, childcare, and ranch duties occur every morning and every evening. Ceremonies and celebrations occur frequently during the weekends. Making time for continuous education is difficult. Therefore, colleges and universities must understand that it is critical to bring educational programs to nearby communities to allow Diné people the opportunity to access college courses, such as teacher preparation classes, certifications, and degrees.

Fort Lewis College responded to the need for more Navajo teachers more than twenty-five years ago by offering Saturday courses during the school year, offering two courses per semester, including summer semesters (every other Saturday), for a two-year period that would allow a teacher aide or community member with an associate's degree to complete the program within a reasonable timeframe. The outreach program offered these Saturday programs in multiple cohorts across the Navajo Nation, including in Shiprock (Central Consolidated School District), Crownpoint, and Farmington. In addition, more than two hundred certified teachers received their TESOL endorsement through Wednesday evening and Saturday courses. The ability to offer programs to teacher aides and individuals who already lived near local schools, and had significant Diné cultural and language backgrounds, has helped schools implement more Navajo language and culture programs.

EMBED NAVAJO CULTURE AND LANGUAGE INTO THE PROGRAM

A second critical feature of the Fort Lewis College Teacher Outreach Program is the emphasis on Navajo culture and language. Part of the coursework required for the bachelor of arts in bicultural studies are Diné College courses in Navajo Language, Teaching Navajo as a Second Language, Navajo Oral History, Navajo Tribal Government, and other specialized courses available at the main campus in Tsaile, or at the satellite campuses in Chinle, Shiprock, Crownpoint, Window Rock, Tuba City, Aneth, and Newcomb. These courses helped reinforce language and culture content for students in the program and would transfer eighteen credits to Fort Lewis College that counted toward the 120 needed for graduation.

In addition, Fort Lewis College coursework built on Diné College courses as candidates progressed through the cohort. By introducing Foundations of Navajo Culture and other courses at Diné College, students could apply Fort Lewis College's courses in lesson planning and curriculum development. For example, the Fort Lewis College course Multicultural Reading and Literacy would complement the previous Diné College course Navajo Oral History, which provided excellent background for reading and writing assignments. Finally, the Diné College course Navajo Tribal Government was critical for the Fort Lewis College Teaching Math and Social Studies course. This sequence allowed students to experience the cyclical nature of learning and scaffolding of concepts.

FLEXIBILITY

Fort Lewis College cohort-based programs were designed with a high degree of flexibility in program design, coursework, and timelines. Once a student started the Fort Lewis College Teacher Outreach Program with ED 490 Education in Indian Country, teacher candidates could take Fort

Lewis College Saturday courses and/or Diné College courses. One student may move rather quickly through the program over two years, while another student might take several years, depending on family and career commitments.

Fort Lewis College coursework also allowed for significant flexibility in designing projects to fit the grade level, location, and subject area of the students in the program. For example, a literacy assignment could be completed in Head Start, fourth grade, a secondary classroom, or a special education classroom, depending where the teacher aide was working.

In summary, the lessons of the Fort Lewis College Teacher Outreach can be valuable to other college and university partnerships with school districts interested in developing "grow your own" models of teacher preparation. The advantages of bringing courses and programs to local communities help to balance educational opportunities with family responsibilities and commitments. The ability to partner with other tribal colleges' efforts ensures culture and language concepts are an essential part of teacher preparation curriculum. The design of the program must include enough flexibility to complete it quickly if time allows but also create a system in which a candidate can drop out and return if other obligations arise. Finally, it is important to provide the support necessary to understand and navigate the Western style of education in order to move toward a more Indigenous style of education in the future.

PART III

PERSPECTIVES OF DINÉ EDUCATIONAL SOVEREIGNTY ACROSS GENERATIONS

CHAPTER 13

NITŁ'IZGO YIISTŁÓ / WOVEN STRONG

The Power of Community-Led Education

LYLA JUNE JOHNSTON

I AM OF the Naaneesht'ezhi Tachii'nii clan of the Diné Nation. I have stud-
ied anthropology as well as language, literacy, and sociocultural studies
with a concentration in American Indian education. I am currently pursuing a doctoral degree focusing on the intersection of Indigenous food
systems and Indigenous land management. As a part of my ongoing focus
on Indigenous community-led education, in the winter of 2015 I initially
convened thirty-five Diné parents, teenagers, and elders and co-founded
Diné Bina'nitin Dóó O'hoo'aah (The People's Teaching and Learning)
with them. I was influenced by my mentors Vincent Werito (Diné) and
Greg Cajete (Tewa), as well as educational philosophers like Paulo Freire,
Trisha Moquino (Kewa), and Glenabah Martinez (Diné/Tiwa).

INTRODUCTION

We can create schools that ignite and harness the ample strengths of
our Indigenous communities. We can create schools that re-center our
language and culture as primary sources of wisdom, knowledge, and
skill-building. We can redefine student success according to our ancestral standards and create places for this knowledge to be leveraged. We

can find creative funding solutions that enable us to teach what we want, how we want, without strings attached. We can shape the destiny of our nations by reclaiming the way our children are educated. We can perpetuate our languages. We can perpetuate our food systems. We can do whatever we set our minds to when we come together as a unified force. Our traditional ways of meeting, praying, gathering, and deciding are prime venues for these important planning and implementation processes.

Diné Bina'nitin Dóó O'hoo'aah is a living example of how all these things are possible. We are a seasonal school designed by community members to achieve our own objectives. We teach everything from *táchééh* (sweathouse) construction, to blue corn recipes, to moccasin making, to weaving, to permaculture, to hogan construction. We are a community that teaches and learns what we want, when we want, how we want, and has a lot of fun doing it. We are self-funded and play by no rules but our own. We are located all throughout Dinétah as a decentralized school. We go wherever people want us. Through this mobile teaching and learning method, we weave *k'é*—community connections and friendships—that makes us a stronger and more joyful nation. We were created by the people, for the people according to our traditional frameworks. We center ceremony, community, and sustainability and are not afraid to be who and what we are as Diné people. We are Diné Bina'nitin Dóó O'hoo'aah, where everyone's voice matters and everyone is a leader—from the smallest child to the wisest elder.

The following chapter details (1) the paradigm shift our school embodies, (2) the way this manifested over the past two years, and (3) some ideas and recommendations for Diné education in general. We hope it serves not only our nation, but all nations in their endeavors to work together for a healthy future.

PARADIGM SHIFT(S)

REDEFINING SUCCESS

Diné Bina'nitin Dóó O'hoo'aah is not a charter school. We are not a public school. We are not a private school. We do not play by any Western rules, and we do not pander to the standards laid out for Indigenous peoples by the colonial state. We are not concerned with our "rankings" according to state departments of education. What we are concerned with is whether or not we have made our elders proud. We are concerned with how we measure up in the face of the teachings of our medicine bundles. Have we succeeded according to the standards of our ancestors? According to the values and principles embedded in our ceremonies, stories, and language? Have we prioritized these things? If so, then we have succeeded in our attempts to educate our mind, voice, body, and spirit.

REDISCOVERING OUR AGENCY AND UNLEARNING POWERLESSNESS

We are an experiment in community-driven education solutions. At the heart of this experiment is the conviction that we can find answers to solve our own problems. We draw on the ample strengths in the Diné community and honor the intelligence, wisdom, and abilities of our language and culture.

In order to create this school, we needed to unlearn powerlessness. It is not our fault as Diné people that we think we are powerless. It is the result of five hundred years of horrific torture by both English and Spanish forces. We need to help each other out of this position we were forced into, and we need to help each other understand how to get out of it. We need to be patient and loving with each other as we rediscover our collective ability to change the world around us.

Here is one famous example of how powerlessness is learned: in circus communities, they noticed that elephants could be trained to imprison themselves. They chain elephants' legs to the ground from a very young age, when they aren't strong enough to break free. The elephant is too small to break free for enough time to believe that they will never break free. When the elephants grow and are strong enough to break free, they are under the illusion that they cannot and don't even try.

In other words, if we are imprisoned from birth, it trains the brain to believe imprisonment is the only reality available to us, even when a new reality opens up. It is difficult to dream up a freedom we've never felt, much less live it. Even when we are released, we do not know how to live and be free, as imprisonment has become a part of our identity. Without that false identity, we have a hard time discovering who we really are.

This is how we end up in a situation where a community has ample power to change their fate and their situation yet remains stagnant. This is not because we do not have the power to change it, but because we have been trained to believe we have no power to change it, through many centuries of horrible war tactics. This is simply not true. We could change things overnight if we had a glimpse of our true power.

The boarding school system has, in many cases, chained us to the belief that "education" comes from the outside world in. We are encouraged as children to "go out" and get an education and bring it "back in." We forfeit our right to educate our own children to outsiders who don't know the first thing about *iiná* (life) and who actively destroy it. Oftentimes, the priceless curriculum embedded in our culture, stories, ceremonies, and languages goes into atrophy or loses value for the children. We never stop to think that maybe what the world really needs is for Diné teachings to be exported outward to heal a broken planet. We never stop to debunk the myths that we are uncivilized and the Western world is not primitive. For nothing is more primitive than poisoning your own water source, which the Western world does day in and day out. Nothing is more barbaric than using this life to dominate others rather than uplift. *Nihizaad*, our language, teaches us to unify and lift each other up, while English teaches us to divide and conquer one another. In some cases (certainly not all), we have forgotten our inherent power to educate ourselves and the world on things that matter to *us*.

Diné Bina'nitin Dóó O'hoo'aah is a bold and courageous exploration into an identity that is so old it is new: the belief that we are able, the belief that we are strong, the belief that we are qualified, and the belief that our knowledge is important.

PEOPLE POWER

Other elements of colonial thought we had to unlearn are (1) the way of the lone wolf and (2) the way of the president and vice president. We are taught in American society that our honor comes from what we can do on our own. The pull-yourself-up-by-the-bootstraps mentality teaches children to be independent instead of collaborative, competitive instead of synergistic. As I will describe below, our school managed to bring one hundred Diné youth, parents, and elders together during the last unit. In the span of four days we built an entire male hogan from bottom to top and plastered it as well. It was phenomenal to see so much progress take place in such a short span of time. We owe this to the power of unified community, which our ancestors practiced and understood very well.

The president/vice president paradigm also desperately needs to be erased. The current Navajo Nation government is an imposed colonial system. It mirrors Congress and the White House. In this system, decisions are made from the top downward. We forfeit our decision-making power to elected individuals who may or may not end up representing the true wishes of the people. This concentrates power in the hands of a few, leaving the majority out of decisions that affect them the most.

A better paradigm is the paradigm of the woven rug—each of us represented by a strand of yarn. The rug depends on every strand to exist, and no strand is more or less important than another. While our contributions and colors may vary, that diversity is leveraged to create beautiful patterns that could never be made by one strand alone. In this paradigm, the leader's job is to convene and bring out the colors of each strand. A leader's role is to facilitate a space where the people's wishes can be expressed, remembered, implemented, evaluated, and re-created. Leaders are weavers of the various strengths of the community.

RE-CENTERING OUR CURRICULUM

In her doctoral work, Glenabah Martinez (Diné/Tiwa; 2010) interviewed Indigenous high school students at a public school in Albuquerque. Students saw the Native studies class offered at their school as a "nonessential elective." They prioritized "harder," "core" classes such as Eurocentric chemistry and mathematics. Native students themselves believed in their languages and cultures, but still saw our own knowledge as less valuable in the grand scheme of things. When I read her study, I was dumbfounded and heartbroken. How have we come to a place where even our own children see our knowledge as "less important" and "nonessential"? I will be the first to admit that when I was going to Taos High School, they offered a Native studies course and I never took it. I was fully indoctrinated in the belief that my honors and AP classes were the foundation that would bring me to "success."

Yet, all around us the evidence is piling up that a world founded on Western ways of "knowing" is a world unraveling. It has generated many "experts" and doctors, yet for some reason cannot generate a solution to wealth disparity. It has generated astronauts and rocket scientists, but still so much war and chaos ravage the planet we live on now. The human-centric, reductionist, racist, materialistic American curriculum has failed to generate a population that can adequately sustain ecological, social, and inner harmony. It has generated plenty of knowledge, but a nation devoid of wisdom.

For these reasons and more, we brought about thirty Diné people together to re-center our grandmothers' wisdom as the root of curriculum development. Our parents were told their knowledge was worthless in the boarding schools, and some of them believed it. We set out to break that cycle and elevate our knowledge as the sophisticated and critically needed science that it is.

FUNDING SWITCH

Yet another essential paradigm shift relates to funding. As Alfred (Kanien'kehá:ka/Mohawk Nation) states, "First Nations today are characterized as entrenched dependencies, in physical, psychological and financial terms, on the very people and institutions that have caused the near erasure of our existence" (2009, 42). A lot of Diné education funding over the past 150 years has come from the American government, an illegal military occupation of Indigenous lands. Thus, our funding comes from the same place that attempted to destroy our languages, culture, and bodies. As in domestic violence, it is not helpful to be financially dependent on an abuser. There will always be subtle conditions and stipulations attached with any assistance we gain from these sources. Reyhner and Eder remind us that U.S. Secretary of the Interior Carl Schurz "issued regulations in 1880 that 'all instruction must be in English' in both mission and government schools under threat of losing government funding" (2004, 76). Three years later Schurz threatened a school to stop teaching the Dakota language or else children would be taken away and funding withdrawn (Reyhner and Eder 2004, 76). Today it takes the form of "Common Core standards," which are no less violent to our epistemologies and cultural identity. These standards hold funding and accreditation hostage until schools assimilate to Eurocentric curricular norms.

Our school found two solutions to this funding conundrum: (1) decrease our need for funding and (2) be strategic about funding sources. An elder once told me, "You don't need much money to do Creator's work." Money cannot buy the most essential things. It can't buy healing. It can't buy community. It can't buy wisdom. It can't buy willpower. *Béeso* (the Diné word for money) is a borrowed term from the Spanish word "peso," meaning "weight" or "coin." We had to borrow this concept because we never needed it before. If we didn't need it then, do we really need it now? Our school functioned quite well, educating over four hundred students in a span of two years, requiring less than $10,000 to do so.

To cut costs, we utilized preexisting classrooms, primarily Nihimá Nahasdzáán, Our Mother Earth. It did not cost money to work together to plant fruit trees for the elders. Much of the materials were supplied by Mother Earth herself or were drawn from materials we possessed as a community. At the same time, until we grow all our own food, we had to buy food to cook lunch and dinner for teachers and participants. This is a way to make it more comfortable and enjoyable for all involved. Thus, we balanced creating a low-budget school with creative funding strategies to host our humble yet life-changing teachings.

We also do not need to be afraid of money. It can enable our dreams for now. It becomes important to be strategic in how you obtain that funding. Sometimes schools need funding quickly and consistently. Moreover, they need to be funded in ways that liberate their programs, not constrict them.

Our school solved these issues with the cunning use of online crowdfunding. The worldwide protest of the Dakota Access Pipeline from 2016 to 2017 is proof that countless people around the world are ready to stand behind Indigenous people. Enough people believe in our way that funding these types of schools is exceedingly simple. It usually took about two hours to make a short film explaining our cause. After uploading it to an online crowdfunding platform, the required funding usually came within a few days. The challenging part is creating a worthy cause and being able to tell its story. If your school does not have the skills to tell the story via social media, there are many people sympathetic to our issues who are more than willing to help.

For larger education projects (e.g., those that require more than $10,000 per month), there are philanthropist organizations. Many exist to help decolonizing/indigenizing efforts circumvent the financial oppression of Indigenous movements. Even if your immediate neighbors are discouraging (or even hostile) toward your curriculum, do not feel alone. The world has an ocean of support that understands the urgency of uplifting Indigenous-led education efforts. Continue to reach out for the help. Connect internationally through online resources. The call will be answered. The world is waiting for Indigenous leaders who can articulate the vision. Once that is provided, the money flows readily. Most importantly, we should never feel pressured to change our dreams in order to get funding.

BRINGING THE SACRED BACK

The final paradigm shift I wish to discuss is allowing for the sacred to guide us once again. In Western education, it is almost taboo to weave prayer and ceremony into the classroom experience. In our people's world, however, life is prayer. There is no specified church because everywhere we go is a place of prayer. Our school is no exception. It is conceived in prayer; it is committed in prayer, and *hataałiis* (medicine people) supervise the learning process. The sacred hogan is a metaphor for our school, as it is an expression of our ancestral epistemology. It is the root of learning, the womb from which we came. We can all pretend that this is not who we are, but at the end of the day, the hogan itself is a sacred place and anything that occurs within is necessarily a sacred process.

A FLOWER BLOOMS

We decided we will define success instead of letting our abuser decide it for us. We decided we are strong and indeed have the power to create the world we want for our children. We decided that the direction of the school will be decided by the teachers and students themselves. We decided to be a collaborative force, instead of self-sufficient. We decided our language and culture were not disposable—that they were the root of our curriculum. We also decided we could fund our program without compromising it. We decided our learning was indeed a sacred process. What happens when we enact these paradigm shifts?

For us, it manifested as a long and careful community planning process. We met every solstice and equinox to create our school based on the Nitsáhákees-Nahat'á-Iiná-Sihasin (Thinking-Planning-Living-Assuring) creation process. The people's beautiful dreams poured forth, and we showed ourselves how creative and brilliant we really are. Together we imagined, planned, implemented, and reflected on community-generated curricula.

During the first planning cycle, the people chose to focus on the following curricular content areas in order of popularity: Ch'iiyaan/Kéyah, (Food/Land), Adá' Akowhiindzin (Identity), Diné Bizaad (Our Language), Diné Baa Hane' (Creation Story), Nayéé' (Assaults on Our Land and People), Chaha'oh/Hoghan (Architecture), Hatáál Dóó Sódizin (Songs and Prayers), K'é (Principles of Kinship), Táchééh (Sweat Lodge), Diyogi (Weaving), Tó (Water), Łíí' (Horse Knowledge), Treaties/Government, Healing Trauma, Traditional Crafts, and Digital Media.

Our first major co-creation was the Four Worlds Summer School. It was named by a single mother who did not have a high school diploma. What she did have was knowledge about our Creation Story and how it helps the people learn. Thus, we framed our school as a four-part learning journey, mirroring the Creation Story.

One of my favorite lessons was the sheepskin tanning workshop. An elder from Fort Defiance, Arizona, came with two hides to show us the way. What I liked about it was how many students worked on the same project. In many Western schools, each student is responsible for their own grade and sits isolated at their own desk. In our school, ten students were kneeling on the earth, exfoliating the same hide with rough rocks, the success of each person depending on the success of other students. The group learning method really reflected our appreciation for k'é: kinship, respect, love, and community connection. One of our students came to a later class to show us hides he tanned on his own using these same methods.

The capstone course of the first Four Worlds Summer School was male hogan construction. None of us had built one before. In partnering with the Black Mesa Water Coalition, we built a male hogan in just four days. Over one hundred Diné students traveled to the base of Sisnaajini, our

Eastern Sacred Mountain, to complete this feat together. Our collaboration did the impossible while at the same time reestablishing Diné presence in an area where we had been historically massacred and driven out. The hogan still stands today as a safe place for any Diné person (or non-Diné for that matter) to come and pray.

Thus, the manifestation of the people's self-driven pedagogy is socially, intellectually, spiritually, and pragmatically potent. The instructional practice that emerges in this liberated space is (among other things) intergenerational, geographically decentralized, experiential, community-sufficiency (instead of self-sufficiency) focused, ceremonial, ecological, traditional, communal, place based, kinship based, consensual, synergistic, healing, gendered, skills/craft based, practical, outdoor, popular, methodical, systematic, seeding/growing community leaders, community led, community sustained, engaging, easier to implement due to shared leadership and responsibility, and mobile.

RECOMMENDATIONS

First, it is important to design curricula that build self-esteem and cultural esteem. If we spend the whole class learning Eurocentric subject matter through Eurocentric instructional methods, what are we really saying to our children? They will begin to internalize the idea that our people's subjects and ways of teaching are not very important.

Second, it is important to look around us and within us for the guiding light. Article IV of the Fort Sumner treaty states: "In order to insure the civilization of the Indians entering into this treaty, the necessity of education is admitted" (Wilkins 2013, 244). This article forced our children into Eurocentric schools to be educated. Since that day, we have internalized the lie that education comes from "others" and not from our elders. But if the Western world has all the answers, why is their world falling apart at the seams? If our world doesn't have the answers, then why is there so much beauty and strength in our language?

Finally, and most importantly, it is time for us to center the hogan instead of centering the colonial state. Shicheii, Donald A. McCabe (Áshįįhii), was the president of Diné College in the 1970s. Raised in Christian boarding schools, he believed his job was to teach Diné students to be more American. Perhaps that is why he held the position for only two years. But what if our task is not to "outdo" the American at his own game and excel in his school of thought? What if our task is to do what Mother Earth needs us to do, what our Creation Stories teach us to do, and what the medicine bundles guide us to do, regardless of what the colonial state is up to? It is true, we do not live in a vacuum but are enmeshed in a big, beautiful world. But, we can learn about the world and communicate with the world while still keeping the hogan fire burning strong. We can be rooted in the soil of Dinétah and still grow our tassels high into the sky. We are not here to be taught by the Western world. We tried that for five hundred years, and it has only brought chaos and destruction to our land and people. On the contrary, we are here to teach the Western world. We are here to help bring the world back to health and *hózhǫ́* once again.

REFERENCES CITED

Alfred, G. T. 2009. "Colonialism and State Dependency." *Journal of Aboriginal Health* 5 (2): 42–60.

Martinez, G. 2010. *Native Pride: The Politics of Curriculum and Instruction in an Urban Public School*. New York: Hampton Press.

Reyhner, J., and J. Eder. 2004. *American Indian Education: A History*. Norman: University of Oklahoma Press.

Wilkins, D. E. 2013. *The Navajo Political Experience*. Lanham, MD: Rowman and Littlefield.

CHAPTER 14

INDIGENIZING PUBLIC EDUCATION

Toward a Diné-Centered Educational Model

DUANE "CHILI" YAZZIE

A LL OF my school years through high school were spent in the public school system. We were enrolled in school because we had to get a white man's education. My parents did not have a choice. I certainly did not have a choice. It was compulsory education required by law. For a few reasons it was a good thing; it filled my days, I was out of my mom's way for a few hours, I got a free meal, I learned new things, and I made new friends. Considering the peripheral benefits, public education is a positive thing at least to that extent.

Where this circumstance becomes debatable is when we critically examine the pronouncement that we needed to "get educated to become a productive member of society." This being the American (Western) societal way that was imposed on us and whose norms we were compelled to conform to. Because we were made prisoners of war and relegated to reservation life and subjected to federal laws, we are expected to accept that we will be told how we will think and how we will live. The American public education program is a foremost example of the colonizers presuming to know better what is good for us, regardless of what we think and believe.

The Creator gave us cultural ways with norms that are separate and different at the foundational level from Western society. Our cultural ways define who we are; they define our individual tribal identities and who we are supposed to be as Indigenous peoples. We have been forced and coerced to sacrifice our Creator-blessed individualism to acquiesce to a compulsory process to be acceptable members of the dominant society. Our inherent life values and Indigenous (Diné) worldview are disrespected. Most certainly, we have standing and justification to question this circumstance. And we must.

The philosophy of the public education that has been imposed on Indigenous peoples is a microcosm of the greater strategy of white dominion over non-white peoples. The roots of this philosophy are traced back to the time when the American government and society decided that Indigenous peoples could not be eradicated and continued through the time when the determination was made to assimilate us, to maneuver us out of our "savagery," and re-mold us into "good Americans." This strategy is reflected in the immoral immortalized words of Richard Henry Pratt, the founder of the Carlisle Indian Industrial School: "Kill the Indian, save the man."

We perpetually mourn the devastating time of kidnapping and being confined in boarding schools, the time of devastating deprivation of family and home, the time of corporal punishment and death for speaking our tongue and honoring our Indigenous ways (Adams 1995; Reyhner 2018). It has been documented that over 150,000 Indian children were subjected to this time of great sadness. Approximately three thousand died away from their homes. There are many more whose fates will always remain unknown.

A uniqueness we have as humankind is the instinct to adapt and determine our best course in life. This instinct is complete with knowing that adaptation and determination should be on one's own terms. Because Westernized education has been and remains a forced proposition on Indigenous people, that uniqueness has been contravened. We were not at the table to define the educational program that would be programmed into the minds and lives of our children. Many of our ancestor grandparents spiritually opposed and physically fought the program of forced education to no avail.

The intents of public education for Indigenous communities remain more consistent with the forced assimilation program of the early church and government. The curricular subject matter is part of a continued deliberate process of indoctrination into the American way and society. We who question this form of indoctrination are concerned with this continued effort at assimilation; it is a blatant affront to our Indigenous identity and our roles and responsibilities in life.

This process of forced public education, which has been and remains a tool of colonialism, has failed to destroy our indigeneity. It has left us in a confusing world of contradictions, conflicting norms, and a clash of values. We have had to redefine our place in our natural world and how best to fit in the modern unnatural world. This adjustment of life has been predicated by the sense of priority for our own families while concurrently retaining our Creator-given identity.

The fact that this system of education continues to fail us is validated by higher rates of truancy, school dropouts, low graduation rates, and the less-than-adequate levels of success of many of our students in universities and colleges. This failure is further demonstrated by the dismal levels of "educational achievement" of many of our students as they come out of secondary school, necessitating the need for those students to get remedial education to have a chance of success in higher education institutions.

When we have questioned the structure and content of the curriculum, the New Mexico Public Education Department (NMPED) has made overtures to correct the problem, but it has not been to the terms and expectations of the Native community. Such overtures have been sporadic and piecemeal; we have had to struggle for whatever gains we may have made. The recognition of the fallacies of public education led Indigenous communities to consider alternative processes of education, such as the Shiprock Alternative School that was founded in 1978, principally by Larry Emerson and Carl Levy. I had the privilege of serving on the inaugural school board along with other Diné grassroots thought leaders of Indian education. The school's philosophy of honoring and using Indigenous-centered teachings on life determined the curriculum, orientation of staff, and treatment of students. This successful venture transformed into the Shiprock Associated Schools Inc. (NiHa'Alchini Ba Educational Center 1985).

The decision of the Yazzie/Martinez case is of momentous import and should make for a resounding and permanent paradigm shift. Unfortunately, it appears the response effort has been mostly a chance to put more funds toward the same process with the faulty design of a top-down strategy of culture subjugation. The champions of the effort at attempting this foundational change in the public education process of Indigenous children are merely attempting to reform a failing system, which rather requires a systemic rebuild with Indigenous education leaders and grassroots thinkers at the table who view life through our true sovereignty and original Indigenous life purpose.

The Yazzie/Martinez case is a clear opportunity for the Indigenous community to state its case for the paradigm shift, but I suspect that all will "play it safe," from the Indigenous leadership and educators to the high echelons of the state government. Even if the Indigenous leaders and educators stand with the courage to advocate that systemic change, it is doubtful the state-level politicians and bureaucracy would loosen or sever the chains of colonialism and shed the false notion of them knowing better what is best for us. Nevertheless, kudos to the Yazzie mom who brought about these realizations and opportunity.

It is necessary that fundamental changes be made in the public education process, and the process of reformatting this education process needs to be done through our Indigenous lens. Our children must know their place in the great creation and their intrinsic relationship to all of the Earth and cosmic energies, that they are of utmost value as beautiful creations and children of the Almighty Creator and the Earth Mother.

The assertion of our true sovereignty as Diné (Navajo Nation) would dictate that it is us who must decide the process of education for our children if we are to truly determine our own destiny.

The sovereignty we assert must be in harmony with the precepts of the inherent sovereignty that we have possessed since the time of our creation. The Diné Customary Law (of the Diné Fundamental Law) declares and teaches that

A. It is the right and freedom of the people that there always be holistic education of the values and principles underlying the purpose of living in balance with all creation, walking in beauty and making a living; and

B. It is the right and freedom of the people that our children are provided with education to absorb wisdom, self-knowledge, and knowledge to empower them to make a living and participate in the growth of the Navajo Nation.

There is no adequate basis for comparison between our Indigenous sovereignty and that of the federal government or the states, because of their different origins. American-style sovereignty is one conceived by man. Our sovereignty is not man conceived and is therefore not subject to being blessed or ratified by any earthly power. It is an absolute imperative that we think, believe, and act from this perspective when considering our future.

One fundamental do-over of the public education process of our Indigenous children will be to incorporate a program that will establish a foundation in preparation for the formal education of each child, wherein the first two years of the enrolled educational process will be spent on orientating the children to the realities of their Indigenous world and the bigger world. This time will be spent on ensuring that the students have instilled in their lives a foundation of the values of dignity, humility, honor, compassion, courage, and respect. Our children must know their individuality and humanity before they are immersed into set curriculums for their formal education careers. These times of teaching will also have the children understand the necessity of being safe and living a healthy life.

Our children must be grounded in all respects; they must understand, claim ownership of, and represent their identity as Indigenous children. This orientation immersion will guide them to understand their identity as precious Indigenous children and human beings; this will lead to their knowing that they have a specific life purpose. They need to know their roles in life and in the world and their responsibility to themselves, to their family, the community, and their tribal nations. They must realize that they are expected to live up to the role and responsibilities they are born for.

One core problem with public education is the "cookie-cutter" approach that assumes the curriculum is good for all children. It assumes the children should all move together toward the common goal of comprehending the teaching, getting good grades, and making it to graduation day. This may be the greatest wrong being perpetrated; to treat all children the same. This treatment is tantamount to the mistreatment of children, as it denies their uniqueness as separate human beings; it denies attention to their individual characteristics, special talents, and separate physical, mental, and emotional needs.

Assessment instruments need to be designed that will give indications of a child's aptitude and interests during the two years of life orientation. These initial assessments can be determinants of the course of study concentration that would be appropriate for each child. As individuals we all have a special talent, an interest in life that is unique to us. We cannot think that a child has limited capacity to express their talents and interests, just because of their young age and having had limited exposure to the world. They are all precious individuals who deserve the opportunity to indicate their interest and thereby be provided all the pertinent educational means for them to develop and amplify their interest and innate talents. They deserve to choose what life they will have in the future.

Partly based on their indicated interest and in consultation with their parents/guardians, the child can be enrolled in a specific educational track; there are four separate tracks that could be considered, which are vocational, cultural, Warrior Way, and academic. This is a response to the cookie-cutter approach of expecting each child to learn the same subject matter in their earlier years of education. It is nonsensical to require a student to learn about medieval European history and other subjects that have no relevance to the world of the young Indigenous student or the world that awaits them.

Students are always being prodded to be a doctor, a lawyer, an astronaut, etc., but they need to be allowed to choose what they want to be in life—it is their life. Adults do a disservice to them by imposing our own preferences and bias on them. As a result, they are not given the respect or honored for the special creations they are.

Vocational—it is well established that Indigenous peoples are "good at working with their hands." Vocational trades are honorable trades, and they are as satisfying as other career options. In many cases, a child wishes to be like their mom, their dad, a grandparent, or a relative in the work they do. We need carpenters, mechanics, welders, and the myriad other professions that the child may want to pursue. To restrict them to a set curriculum they may have no interest in harms, confuses, and frustrates them; it deters them from reaching their potential and perhaps prevents them from finding their true purpose in life.

Cultural—undoubtedly there are children who recognize the value and necessity of remaining who they were made to be as Indigenous people. There are those who are attuned to the natural and Native lifestyle where the Native language is spoken, where the customary traditions are practiced including the ceremonial ways of the people. It is urgently necessary that our cultural values and traditions be kept and the most natural way of doing that is the teaching of these ways to the children, most preferably from a young age.

Warrior Ways—in our Indigenous societies, the Warrior role is prominent and of utmost importance, a structured course of study will be developed that is rooted in the Indigenous concepts of the Warrior Way. This course of study will be geared toward a career in firefighting, police, the military, or other public safety interests. They would fill the ranks of the ROTC or like programs and other relevant training processes.

Academic—we have our cadre of students who are driven to achieve and to be that lawyer, doctor, or scientist. These students need to be provided every resource and given absolute and consistent support in their academic pursuits. They must be given every appropriate opportunity to excel and to challenge the world as the brightest and formally achieving representation of our great Indigenous people.

With the exercise of our tribal sovereignty, the public education regime also needs to be advised what our preferences are for a school year schedule that aligns with the needs and practices of our people, communities, and nations. Many of our Indigenous teachings revolve around the seasons of the year, and it is feasible to design the education process to afford them the experience and exposure to the traditional cultural teachings based on the seasons. One consideration that will be a determinant in the setting of the school calendar year is the commencement of the Indigenous new year, which for the Diné begins the first of October.

The school year scheduling would also incorporate local preferences including the farming community needs: a significant component of the education study time can be focused on a schedule coinciding with the agricultural growing season. This would suggest that the school year schedule would be based on the need to include the farmlands' preparation time from the early spring months through the harvest season of the fall months. The teachings around agriculture are critical and of great importance.

Another aspect on reprogramming the school year would be that, rather than having continual nine-month school years with holiday and spring breaks, there would be month-long non-school times during the holidays and a month of break time at two other strategic points in the calendar year. This would facilitate a continuous teaching and learning process with shortened intervals of break time. These break times could include projects that are classroom relevant to consistently enhance the education process and keep the student's interest.

A final concern that has tremendous impact on the education of Indigenous children is teacher certification requirements. NMPED is having to recruit degreed teachers from foreign lands due to the shortage of teachers. It is ludicrous that recruitment of foreign teachers is felt necessary when our students have a problem in understanding the heavily accented verbalization of foreign teachers. This constitutes a further divergence from a meaningful educational process that is of critical necessity for the children to find their futures. NMPED needs a serious reality check.

There needs to be a review of teacher certification requirements to fit the changing circumstances. This would be requisite to accommodate the changes we propose in the public education system, particularly in the incorporation of the four separate education tracks. It will not be necessary to have degreed teachers to teach certain subject areas of the four separate tracks of learning but to have teachers who possess expertise in various subject matter that will be relevant to the child's education within a nonacademic learning track. The community and tribal nations must determine who will teach our children.

In the sincere interest of providing the optimum of education of our students, there must be objective consideration and dialogue between all pertinent stakeholders. After all, our intent is to ensure that our children are afforded a complete education that will give them the optimum opportunity to succeed in achieving their life dreams.

REFERENCES CITED

Adams, D. W. 1995. *Education for Extinction: American Indians and the Boarding School Experience, 1875–1928.* Lawrence: University Press of Kansas.

NiHa'Alchini Ba Educational Center. 1985. *To Sing Our Own Songs: Cognition and Culture in Indian Education: Report from a Workshop for American Indian Educators on the Learning Potential Assessment Device and Instrumental Enrichment*

Programs, Shiprock, Navajo Nation, New Mexico. New York: Association on American Indian Affairs.

Reyhner, J. 2018. "American Indian Boarding Schools: What Went Wrong? What Is Going Right?" *Journal of American Indian Education* 57 (1): 58–78.

CONCLUSION

TOWARD A DINÉ-CENTERED PEDAGOGY FOR TRANSFORMATIVE EDUCATIONAL PRAXIS

VINCENT WERITO AND PEDRO VALLEJO

N THE introductory chapter, we started with a review of the state of Navajo education to highlight its challenges and promises. In this concluding chapter we discuss the need for Diné educational models that underscore past and present innovations in Diné education as presented by this collection of authors. In their own unique ways, these Diné educators and educators of Diné youth embody Diné education through their practices and beliefs by acknowledging the ongoing legacies and remnants of colonization while also recognizing their cultural capabilities, cultural integrity, collective community wealth, resilience, and strengths with the goal of always having hope in the face of challenges.

Despite the repeated attacks on our cultural sovereignty and our human rights as Diné (the People), our ancestors held onto their beliefs, their language, and their way of life by drawing on their resolve to survive using the philosophy and teachings of Sa'ah Naaghái Bik'eh Hózhóón. Due to the resilience of our ancestors, today we have retained our lifeways with the strength of Nihimá Nahasdzáán (our sacred Earth Mother) and *nihizaad* (our sacred language) to sustain *nihina'nitin dóó 'ohoo'aah* (our ancestors' teachings) to perpetuate 'adoone'é niidlínígíí (our sacred bloodlines through clan affiliations) using *k'é* (the acknowledgment of all our relations within the entire universe) to become Sa'ah Naaghái Bik'eh

Hózhǫ́ǫ́n (the children of the Holy People). Today, we are the embodiment and promises of our ancestors' prayers as we continue to persevere and overcome anything just as they did in the past with the guidance of our traditional spiritual ceremonies, prayers, songs, and undying hope and resilience for the benefit of future generations.

This is a story, or precisely a counter-narrative, about the People's ongoing struggles to overcome the past and ongoing processes of colonization and realize a different kind of promise, that of a Diné educational agenda to help realize and reimagine the purposes of education (i.e., seeking knowledge) and what that means to our way of life (for Diné life's sake) as well as its implications for the future, especially for the benefit of our children and grandchildren as they perpetuate and sustain our language, cultural practices, and ways of being/living. By coming to this realization and understanding, we embrace a Diné-centered politics of *hózhǫ́* (Emerson 2014) that is based on our aspirations, goals, hopes, and the possibilities for decolonization, liberation, and transformation to heal our communities, our minds, and our spirits as they come back full circle to our Diné philosophy of education and living (Aronilth 1994). Moving forward, Diné educators must articulate a Diné-centered politics and pedagogy that is premised on achieving critical Diné-centered consciousness and community well-being guided by the earth memory compass (King 2018; Werito and Belone 2021) and our Diné-centered perspectives of education (Aronilth 1992; Werito 2016) within which lie the answers, hopes, promise, and possibilities for transformative praxis that we seek to attain and sustain through our Diné philosophy of education.

In looking ahead to the possibilities and promises of realizing our ancestors' prayers for continuance of our Diné ways of life for our children, in this final chapter we discuss the need for a decolonizing, transformative educational agenda that draws from a politics of hózhǫ́ (Emerson 2014) along with our traditional Diné knowledge/teachings (Aronilth 1994; Austin 2009; McPherson 2012) to articulate a Diné-centered pedagogy to restore our humanity, way of life, language, and identity. As we continue to move beyond critically examining past and present educational laws, policies, practices, and regulations at the tribal, federal, state, and district level that impact Diné education, the significance of Diné Fundamental Laws pertaining to our traditional forms of self-governance (Austin 2009; Diné Bi Beenahaz'áanii [Fundamental Laws of the Diné],

1 Navajo Nation Code §§ 201–206 [http://www.courts.navajo-nsn.gov/dine.htm]) become crucial in our struggle for educational sovereignty. In doing so, we affirm, reclaim, recover, and regenerate the potential and strength of Diné language and thought as a "stand-alone system" (Emerson 2016). Furthermore, we believe there must be a conscious effort to acknowledge the legacies of colonization and to name who we are and tell our stories again using a decolonizing transformative approach that advances a Diné-centered pedagogy intrinsically informed by Diné ways of thinking, living, learning, and being. So, what does this look like? How can we overcome past and present-day challenges and move toward a transformative approach and understanding to create an educational system that works for Diné children in the here and now (Yazzie-Mintz 2008) and the future while drawing on our history and traditional knowledge?

DINÉ-CENTERED PEDAGOGY

According to Diné elders, our philosophy of education was based on the actions, behaviors, and teachings about the Holy People (Aronilth 1992, 1994). For example, one Diné oral tradition tells of how the Holy People delegated Coyote to teach the children of the Holy People:

> The story goes that one day Coyote came across "the People" as they were arguing over who should be responsible for teaching their children when they were off working in the cornfields. Coyote volunteered when no one else would. He said, "I will do it. I know how to teach the children. I will bring them back knowing all the ways and knowledge of the Holy People." After the fourth request and much hesitation, everyone agreed to let him take the children back to his home. Coyote went off with the children. However, he had other intentions in mind. The children remained with Coyote for four days. After four days, when the children returned to "the People," they were undisciplined, manipulative, and deceitful just like Coyote himself. In the end, after much trouble and intervention, it was clear that it was up to the people themselves to teach (and re-teach) their own children what they wanted them to learn. "The People" realized that it was their role and responsibility to teach their own children. So, with the intervention of Talking God, Pollen Boy, Pollen Girl, and the Tobacco people,

the children were finally restored to harmony. Their journey through life's dilemma resulted in the community coming to a realization that they must take responsibility for their own education.

The moral of this story is obvious. It is up to Diné parents, educators, and community members to take responsibility for their own children and their learning. This is the first crucial step to decolonizing our minds and to reclaiming Indigenous forms of education.

In *Power and Place*, Deloria and Wildcat (2001) discuss a critical need to develop Indigenous models of education by centering the history and perspectives of Indigenous peoples in relation to their languages and worldviews. For example, in looking at traditional Indigenous technology—that is, knowledge of plants, animals, and the land—they state that it is important "because it reminds us that we must take our cue about the world from the experiences and evidence that world gives us"(Deloria and Wildcat 2001, 65). Further, Wildcat writes:

> If we human beings begin our understanding of the natural world with the big picture, we must acknowledge our relatively recent arrival to our Mother Earth's biosphere. The result ought to be a kind of biological modesty, for many of our biosphere community members have been here much longer than we have. (Deloria and Wildcat 2001, 77)

In the Diné worldview, the Diyin Dine'é are those who came before such as the primordial life forces (air, water, sunlight, and earth) that constitute all life followed by the Twelve Holy People, the insects, the four-legged, and the winged ones.

According to Diné elders, the Diyin Dine'é (Holy People) created the Diné philosophy of traditional education (Sa'ah Naaghái Bik'eh Hózhǫ́ǫ́n Na'nitin) and Diné language (Diné Bizaad) for the benefit of Ni'hookáá' Diyin Dine'é (Earth Surface people) so they may flourish and thrive in the future (Aronilth 1994). Similarly, Diné elders believe that the Diné language was created in the First World and was the language of the Holy People. Language is considered to be sacred because it is inherent to the life breath of an individual (Aronilth 1992). Over time, it is believed that the Holy People bestowed the gift of language unto the Diné (the People) as the Children of the Holy People. Through previous worlds and finally unto emergence in the Fourth World as told in our journey narratives (Austin 2009), Diné language and cultural teachings have been passed on by word of mouth for many generations through stories, ceremonies, and the traditional teachings of the home, family, and community life.

In the present, educational discussions, research, and practices are needed that draw on the Diné philosophy of education—Sa'ah Naagháí Bik'eh Hózhǫ́ǫ́n—which is often described as our Diné way of life and spiritual journey through life to achieve happiness and reach old age. Benally (1994) writes, "For Diné, knowledge, learning and life itself are sacred and interwoven parts of a whole. They are the holistic principles that determine the quality of each other" (23). The whole being is Sa'ah Naagháí Bik'eh Hózhǫ́ǫ́n, which translates to achieving long life in happiness. This philosophy can encompass language, cultural identity, cultural beliefs, knowledge, and spiritual values. Furthermore, from this paradigm, the assertions of language rights or human rights are not predicated on human ontology but on supernatural laws or Diné Fundamental Laws (Austin 2009), thus making an inherent claim to language and basic human rights for Diné children to learn and speak their heritage language and carry on Diné teachings for many generations to come. In particular, Aronilth (1994) writes that our current Navajo education system should be informed by our cultural knowledge and teachings (pedagogy) because this knowledge is a stand-alone system of knowledge that contains what we know, need, and understand.

At a Diné language revitalization summit in Tsaile, Arizona, Aronilth shared four Diné methods (or principles) of learning based on his grandmother's teachings on how to live according to Sa'ah Naagháí Bik'eh Hózhǫ́ǫ́n (Aronilth 2017). As he shared these methods, he mentioned that many educators and tribal leaders would often only mention the third method of "t'aa hó'ajit'éego," or *it is up to you.* The following list includes the four methods or principles of Diné learning (i.e., pedagogy) as shared by Aronilth along with some of our interpretations.

1. Doo hwil hóyee'dá / "Don't' be lazy"

    In life, starting with each day, you must not be fearful because that can lead to self-doubt, self-pity, and laziness. You must embrace the courage in your heart to face any obstacles that come your way and overcome them with all of your capabilities/strengths. This teaching relates to the process of naming oppression (Freire 2000) through the acknowledgment of the legacies and remnants of education while also affirming the cultural and spiritual strengths of Diné language and education to overcome all obstacles. It recognizes that there are present-day monsters like hunger, poverty, illness, and laziness that need to be defeated on a daily basis to survive and thrive to reach old age in happiness.

2.   T'áá'oolwolíbee / "Use all of your strength and capacities"

Over the span of your lifetime, especially when you are young, you must realize that you have full potential and full capabilities to achieve anything. You must draw on your own strength and full faculties of your mind, body, and spirit because you are very capable of doing anything you want and do not need to always rely on others because the knowledge and wisdom is already within. The principle is related to the concept of transculturation theory defined by Huffman as a "process by which a Native student journeys through a mainstream-dominant education institution while building on his/her tribal identity and heritage while simultaneously learning the cultural nuances necessary to thrive and succeed" (2020, 88). Moreover, the idea expands on the cultural strengths of an individual and community well-being that include the mental, physical, emotional, and spiritual aspects of a person (Werito and Belone 2021). Finally, it emphasizes building on community cultural wealth as the "array of knowledge, skills, abilities, and contacts possessed and utilized by communities of color to survive and resist macro- and micro-forms of oppression" (Yosso 2005, 77).

3.   T'aa hó'ajit'éego / "It's up to you"

Everything you need to know or want to learn is already within, in your mind, body, and spirit. It is up to you to accomplish what you put your mind to because the knowledge is already within you; you just need to draw it out and believe in yourself. This principle relates to the notion of endogenous education, or educating "the inner self through enliven-

ment and illumination from one's own being and the learning of key relationships" (Cajete 1994, 34). Moreover, Indigenous scholar Marie Battiste
writes, "The distinctive features of Indigenous knowledge and pedagogy
are learning by observation and doing, learning through authentic experiences and individualized instruction, and learning through enjoyment.
Indigenous pedagogy accepts students' cognitive search for learning processes they can internalize" (2002, 19).

4.   T'aa 'anííjinízin / "Believe in what you are doing"

Throughout your entire life, you must always have hope and faith in what
you are doing but most importantly, you must believe in it. Every day
should start with prayers so that you continue to believe in yourself, your
language, what you hope to aspire to, and how you want your life to be
within the spirit of k'é and hózhǫ́. Finally, this principle relates to what it
means to be respectful to all things in the universe and how k'é (acknowledging all relationships) informs notions of respect, reciprocity, and trust
through action, reflection, and ongoing interactions with everything in the
universe by invoking the idea of intuition or spirituality (Dei 2002; Cajete
2000), especially in regard to learning.

By affirming these principles of Diné pedagogy, Diné educators re-
center Diné thought, language, ways of knowing, and lifeways that pre-
dated Western education. Diné-centered pedagogy is essential to Diné
youths' attitudes, capabilities, and motivations for learning and a sense
of trust/respect for self within specific cultural and social processes of
learning and teaching. Consequently, a Diné-centered pedagogy starts
with what we already know and practice in our homes, families, and
communities, which are often connected to our lived experiences and
spiritual forms of knowledge and relations/connections to place; that
is, our "pedagogy" as Diné is found in us, in our relationships to each
other, in nature around us, in our spiritual education, and in our origin
stories, which are tied to place and spirit. Thus, our true way to knowing
ourselves and reclaiming our languages is not only found in theory as
constructed by others but through action in our struggle or search to
understand our place in the world (Emerson 2014, 2016).

According to the late Larry Emerson, a politics of Hózhǫ́ can "adequately define the nature of Diné sovereignty, self-determination, and sustainability in these contemporary times" (2014, 66). He goes on to add, "It is best for us to envision a future of peace and harmony and to evolve practices that promote such outcomes. After all, as Diné peoples we have rights to hózhǫ́, or harmony, beauty, balance, peace, and happiness" (Emerson 2014, 66). With regard to reclaiming/reaffirming a uniquely Diné way of teaching and learning, Emerson (2016) states that we need to think and problematize Indigenously about how we understand our relationship with one another, with others, with the United States, and other state governments. In doing so, he posits that we must rearticulate our ways of knowing, being, and thinking that put Indigenous thought at the center of our existence: "We must reclaim our Diné sovereignty law that was here before America, before colonization, before all else. We are Diné!" (Emerson 2016). Moreover, it requires us to *think in Navajo* (Werito 2020) about many critical issues impacting our communities. In doing so, we affirm, reclaim, recover, and revitalize our ways of knowing, our language, and our ways of being that put Diné thought at the center of our existence. A crucial part of this centering involves affirming and utilizing Diné elder knowledge that speaks to the truth of our history and stories (Kelley and Francis 2019; McPherson 2012). Finally, by embracing a Diné-centered pedagogy, we too can learn to speak to the truth of our history and stories so that there is relevance to what children should learn and how they will live and thrive in the future.

Diné-centered pedagogy is inherently and naturally based on the process of learning, living, and teaching paradigms that are central to Sa'ah Naaghái Bik'eh Hózhǫ́ǫ́n and T'áá Shá Bik'ehgo Diné Bí Na'nitin dóó 'Íhoo'aah (Division of Dine Education 2003). The T'áá Shá Bik'ehgo Diné Bí Na'nitin dóó 'Íhoo'aah teachings are literally interpreted to mean "sunwise path teachings." These teachings are based on the relationships between humans and their interactions with and understanding of the natural environment. For many generations, the Diné have observed their unique relationship with the natural environment within their homelands, which are located within four sacred mountains as told in their origin stories, or journey narratives (Austin 2009). The significance of T'áá Shá Bik'ehgo Na'nitin to learning is based on the Diné belief that the sun travels in a clockwise direction starting in the east and ends in its resting place in the north. With this in mind, the Diné believe that humans grow and develop, the four seasons revolve around this sacred cycle, and the natural world lives according to this natural order of the sun's journey through the day, year, and all time. By living in accordance with the Diné philosophy of education, or the Sa'ah Naaghái Bik'eh Hózhǫǫn paradigm based on T'áá Shá Bik'ehgo, or sunwise, teachings, Diné people have and continue to negotiate meaning and identity in relation to the universe, and extending from this unique worldview are their language, stories, songs, and cultural traditions. Also by incorporating new ideas to current realities and yet remaining steadfast to the ideals of the past through rooted identities, the Diné have passed on and will continue to pass on their language and oral traditions for many generations to come. In this way, the Diné philosophy of education or living and learning can be used as model or a process of learning and living by which anyone, regardless of ethnicity, race, class, creed, or religious background, can understand who they are and determine who they want to be in future life.

This creative process of orientation to the natural world for learning, living, and teaching begins with critical thinking followed by the setting of life plans and goals, which is then followed by social life development and finally moving to self-reflection and awareness. By following this cyclic process of learning, teachers and students are actively engaged on a daily basis in a process of new (renewed) learning, setting goals, developing social/emotional skills, and active reflexivity that ultimately leads to critical consciousness (Werito 2014) and sets the stage for social transformation and praxis. In sum, Indigenous educational models and pedagogies are based on Indigenous epistemologies, or ways of knowing and understanding the natural world. They are essentially "research-oriented," creative processes of observing, learning, understanding, and making sense of the world through trial and error or everyday experiences (Aluli Meyer 2003; Cajete 1994, 2000). They are important to understanding the dialogical/dialectical nature of seeking and finding knowledge for life's sake.

In sum, traditionally and in many cases today, the education of Diné children begins with traditional stories that are passed on from previous generations about the home, family, community, and society. Later, as a child grows, these stories and teachings, or Dinéji Na'nitin (McPherson 2012), are applied and extended to everyday practical applications to provide meaning through interactions and lessons learned from and with the extended family, larger community, and world (Aronilth 1992, 1994; Austin 2009; King 2018). These traditional teachings and stories that are learned along with core values and beliefs are carried on and passed on from the elders to youth through our unique pedagogical approaches to understanding who we are as Diné. In this way, a Diné-centered pedagogy (i.e., Diné ways of learning and teaching) is vital to the well-being of young Diné children now and in the future.

REFERENCES CITED

Aluli Meyer, M. 2003. *Hoo'ulu: Our Time of Becoming: Hawaiian Epistemology and Early Writings*. Honolulu, HI: 'Ai Pōhaku Press.

Aronilth, W., Jr. 1992. *Foundation of Navajo Culture*. Tsaile, AZ: Diné College.

Aronilth, W., Jr. 1994. *Diné Bi Bee Óhoo'aah Bá Silá: An Introduction to Navajo Philosophy*. 4th ed. Tsaile, AZ: Diné College.

Aronilth, W., Jr. 2017. "Traditional Perspectives on Navajo Language." Paper presented at the Navajo Language Revitalization Summit, May 22–23, Tsaile, AZ.

Austin, R. D. 2009. *Navajo Courts and Navajo Common Law: A Tradition of Tribal Self-Governance*. Minneapolis: University of Minnesota Press.

Battiste, M. 2002. "Indigenous Knowledge and Pedagogy in First Nations Education: Literature Review with Recommendations." Paper prepared for National Working Group on Education and the Minister of Indian Affairs, Indigenous and Northern Affairs Canada, Ottawa, Ontario.

Benally, H. 1994. "Navajo Philosophy of Learning and Pedagogy." *Journal of Navajo Education* 12 (1): 23–31.

Cajete, G. 1994. *Look to the Mountain: An Ecology of Indigenous Education*. Denver, CO: Kivakí Press.

Cajete, G. 2000. *Native Science: Natural Laws of Interdependence*. Santa Fe, NM: Clear Light.

Dei, G. 2002. "Spiritual Knowing and Transformative Learning." In *Expanding the Boundaries of Transformative Learning: Essays on Theory and Praxis*, edited by E. O'Sullivan, A. Morrell, and M. A. O'Connor, 121–33. New York: Palgrave Macmillan.

Deloria, V., Jr., and D. Wildcat, D. 2001. *Power and Place: Indian Education in America*. Golden, CO: Fulcrum Resources.

Division of Diné Education. 2003. *T'áá Shá Bik'ehgo Diné Bí Na'nitin dóó 'Íhoo'aah* (Diné Cultural Content Standards for Students). Window Rock, AZ: Office of Diné Culture, Language, and Community Services.

Emerson, L. 2014. "Diné Culture, Decolonization, and the Politics of Hózhǫ́." In *Diné Perspectives: Reclaiming and Revitalizing Navajo Thought*, edited by L. Lee, 49–67. Tucson: University of Arizona Press.

Emerson, L. 2016. "Indigenous Language Revitalization: Engaging Confluences, Conflicts, and Contradictions—Where Do We Go from Here?" Paper presented at La Cosecha 22nd Annual National Dual Language Conference, November 9–12, Santa Fe, NM.

Freire, P. 2000. *Pedagogy of the Oppressed*. 2nd ed. New York: Continuum.

Huffman, T. 2020. "Transculturation Theory: a Framework for Understanding Tribal Identity and Academic Success." In *Honoring Our Students*, edited by J. Reyhner, J. Martin, L. Lockard, and W. S. Gilbert, 87–110. Flagstaff: Northern Arizona University.

Kelley, K., and H. Francis. 2019. *A Diné History of Navajo Land*. Tucson: University of Arizona Press.

King. F. 2018. *The Earth Memory Compass: Diné Landscapes and Education in the Twentieth Century*. Lawrence: University Press of Kansas.

McPherson, R. S. 2012. *Dinjéjí Na'nitin: Navajo Traditional Teachings and History*. Boulder: University Press of Colorado.

Werito, V. 2014. "Understanding Hózhǫ́ to Achieve Critical Consciousness: A Contemporary Diné Interpretation of the Philosophical Principles of Hózhǫ́." In *Diné Perspectives: Revitalizing and Reclaiming Navajo Thought*, edited by L. Lee, 25–38. Tucson: University of Arizona Press.

Werito, V. 2016. "Education Is Our Horse: On the Path to Critical Consciousness in Teaching and Learning." In *Going Inward: The Role of Cultural Introspection in College Teaching*, edited by S. D. Longerbeam and A. F. Chávez, 67–73. New York: Peter Lang Publishing.

Werito, V. 2020. "'Think in Navajo': Reflections from the Field on Reversing Navajo Language Shift in the Home, School, and Community Contexts." In *Honoring Our Students*, edited by J. Reyhner, J. Martin, L. Lockard, and W. S. Gilbert, 39–51. Flagstaff: Northern Arizona University.

Werito, V., and L. Belone. 2021. "Research From a Diné-Centered Perspective and the Development of a Community-Based Participatory Research Partnership." *Health Education and Behavior* 48 (3): 361–70.

Yazzie-Mintz, T. 2008. "Creating Culture in the Here and Now: Regenerating Rituals in Purposeful Epistemologies." In *Indigenous Educational Models for Contemporary Practice: In Our Mother's Voice, Volume II*, edited by M. K. P. Ah Nee-Benham, 13–20. New York: Routledge.

Yosso, T. J. 2005. "Whose Culture Has Capital? A Critical Race Theory Discussion of Community Cultural Wealth." *Race, Ethnicity, and Education* 8 (1): 69–91.

CONTRIBUTORS

Berlinda Begay is Diné and her clans are Bit'ahnii, born for Ta'neeszahnii, her maternal grandfather is Kin łichíí'nii, and Áshįįhí is her paternal grandfather's clan. She is a bilingual multicultural education coordinator for Central Consolidated Schools. She was raised in Rock Point, Arizona, and attended Rock Point Community School until ninth grade, and then attended Fountain Valley School, a college-preparatory school, for her remaining high school years. She currently resides on her grandmother's homelands in Red Mesa, Arizona, with her husband Anthony M. Begay and two of her four children. She has over twenty-five years of teaching and administrative experience working with K–12, specifically in Navajo language and culture. Her academic interests have always been Navajo language and culture and currently in culturally responsive teaching. She believes in culturally responsive teaching because she attended Rock Point Community School, a true Navajo bilingual and bicultural school that incorporated Navajo language and cultural education into the curriculum where students excelled academically. She continues to share her knowledge and expertise in Navajo language and culturally responsive teaching as an adjunct faculty for Fort Lewis College. She attributes her Western educational success to her humble upbringing, and it continues to inspire her to do her current work in Navajo language revitalization and preservation and advocacy.

Lorenda Belone, PhD, MPH, is Diné from the community of Naakaii Bito' and a University of New Mexico associate professor within the College of Education and Human Sciences. She is a community-based participatory researcher and currently is principal investigator (PI) of a health implementation study (NIDA-R01, 2020–25) with six Southwest tribal communities and co-PI of a health intervention study (NIDA-R01, 2014–21) with three Southwest tribal communities; she is also the codirector of the UNM Community Engagement and Dissemination Core (NIMHD-U54, 2017–22) and was the co-investigator on a study examining the science of CBPR (NRO-R01, 2015–20).

Michael "Mikki" Carroll is the head of school at a public charter school in Albuquerque, New Mexico. She has worked in education for twenty-plus years as a teacher and administrator. She is currently a doctoral student in the Native American Leadership in Education (NALE) program at the University of New Mexico, College of Education and Human Sciences, which is an all Indigenous cohort. She is from the Diné (Navajo) nation and believes in culturally relevant pedagogies in schools. Part of her work has encompassed the study of school discipline as a former dean of students. She and her team have successfully implemented restorative justice in her school and supported teachers with the approach and continue to develop the model. She has also furthered her research in various Indigenous frameworks and included restorative justice models as part of her work in her dissertation. She is an advocate for effective school policies and practices that align to the cultural identity of students as well as helping tribes with self-determination in their education systems in tribally controlled schools.

Quintina "Tina" Deschenie is Ta'neeszahnii, born for Tó'aheedlíini. Her *cheii* are the Tewa from First Mesa in Arizona, and her *nálí* are Bit'ahnii. She grew up in Crystal, New Mexico, her family home, and in the Becenti community near Crownpoint, New Mexico. She is married to Michael Thompson (Muscogee), a retired educator. She received a BA in business from Fort Lewis College, an MA in education from the University of New Mexico, and an EdD in educational administration from New Mexico State University. She worked in Indian education for nearly thirty years in numerous schools and at the Department of Diné Education. She was also an editor for the *Tribal College* journal and was the first Diné woman provost at Navajo Technical University. She retired as administrator of the Dream Diné Charter School in 2019.

Henry Fowler, EdD, is from Tonalea, Arizona. He is a member of the Navajo tribe. He is an associate math professor at Navajo Technical University in Crownpoint, New Mexico. He is born for Bitter Water and born into the Zuni Edgewater; his maternal grandparents are Many Goats, and his paternal grandparents are Red Running into the Water. He started his formal education at the age of four at Kaibeto Boarding School in Kaibeto, Arizona. He received his bachelor's degree in mathematics education and master's degree in education from Northern Arizona University in Flagstaff and received his EdD in educational leadership and change from Fielding Graduate University in Santa Barbara, California. He has been teaching math for over twenty years and is the cofounder of the Navajo Math Circles. Navajo Math Circles provides teacher workshops for grades K–12 and works with over forty mathematicians to promote math education for students from the Navajo Nation. His research interests lie in the area of ethnomathematics, and he is passionate about promoting math literacy and advocating social justice through mathematics. He strongly supports relevant cultural materials to guide instruction.

Richard Fulton, retired educator, former School of Education dean, Fort Lewis College, in Durango, Colorado, has thirty-seven years of teaching and educational leadership experience in Colorado, primarily focused on working with disadvantaged youth in alternative schools, leading several charter schools, and creating many pre-K–higher education partnerships with diverse educators in the Four Corners region.

Davis E. Henderson, PhD, CCC-SLP, is an assistant professor at Northern Arizona University (NAU) in the Department of Communication Sciences and Disorders. He received his PhD from Arizona State University in 2017. His research of expertise is in the area of Navajo linguistics, Navajo speech and language assessments and development, and psychometrics. At NAU, he is the director of the Indigenous, Culturally and Linguistically Diverse (In-CLD) Language Research Lab.

Kelsey Dayle John (Diné) is an assistant professor at the University of Arizona with a joint appointment in the Departments of American Indian Studies and Gender and Women's Studies. She holds a PhD in cultural foundations of education from Syracuse University. Her work is centered on animal relationalities, particularly horse/human relationships as ways of knowing, healing, and decolonizing education. Alongside her work in Indigenous animal studies, Kelsey's research interests also include Indigenous feminisms, decolonizing methodologies, and Diné studies.

Lyla June Johnston is an Indigenous musician, scholar, and community organizer of Diné (Navajo), Tsétsêhéstâhese (Cheyenne), and European lineages. Her dynamic, multigenre presentation style has engaged audiences across the globe toward personal, collective, and ecological healing. She blends studies in human ecology at Stanford, graduate work in Indigenous pedagogy, and the traditional worldview she grew up with to inform her music, perspectives, and solutions. She is currently pursuing her doctoral degree, focusing on Indigenous food systems revitalization.

Tracia Keri Jojola (Tábąąhí niliigo' dóó Tó'áhaní yásh'chíín. 'Áshįįhí dabicheii dóó Tódích'íi'nii dabinálí. Ákót'éego Diné Asdzáá nilí) is Tábąąhí (the Water Edge People Clan), born for Tó'áhaní (Near the Water Clan), her maternal grandfather was 'Áshįįhí (Salt Clan), and her paternal grandfather was Tódích'íi'nii (Bitter Water Clan) of the Diné (Navajo). She is originally from To'Hajiilee, New Mexico, which is a satellite community of Diné Bikéyah (Navajoland). She is an education program administrator for the Albuquerque Education Resource Center within the Bureau of Indian Education (BIE). She is responsible for the management, oversight, and effectiveness of education programs within bureau-operated schools. In her previous role within the BIE, she worked with tribally controlled schools located across the United States. As an educational professional, with over twenty years of experience, she has spent more than half of her career providing direct services to students as a teacher and school counselor. Once she transitioned into the role of a school administrator, she was able to implement effective practices and advocate for important systemic changes, such as Diné language revitalization. She holds a bachelor's degree in psychology/social welfare, a master's in school counseling, and a doctoral degree in educational administration.

She holds Level III licensure in school administration, teaching (K–8), and school counseling.

Tiffany S. Lee is Dibé Łizhiní (Blacksheep) Diné from Crystal, New Mexico, and Oglala Lakota from Pine Ridge, South Dakota. She is a professor and the chair of the Department of Native American Studies at the University of New Mexico in Albuquerque. Her research examines educational and culturally based outcomes of Indigenous language immersion schools, Native youth perspectives on language reclamation, and socioculturally centered education. Her work has been published in journals, such as the *American Journal of Education, Harvard Educational Review, Journal of Language, Identity, and Education*, and *Journal of American Indian Education*; and in books, such as *Culturally Sustaining Pedagogies: Teaching and Learning for Justice in a Changing World, Diné Perspectives: Revitalizing and Reclaiming Navajo Thought*, and *Indigenous Language Revitalization in the Americas*. She is the former president of the Navajo Studies Conference and a former high school social studies and language arts teacher at schools on the Navajo Nation and at Santa Fe Indian School. She is also a former member of the New Mexico Indian Education Advisory Council for the Office of Indian Education, New Mexico Public Education Department.

Shawn Secatero, PhD, is a member of the Canoncito Band of Navajos and is an associate professor in the University of New Mexico's (UNM) Department of Teacher Education, Educational Leadership, and Policy. His research concentrates on holistic learning, Indigenous leadership, dual enrollment, rural education, and Indigenous education. His research focuses on holistic well-being, which is designed to promote education, healing, and epistemology for Native American and rural communities. He teaches courses in Visionary Leadership, Communications for Leaders, School Finance, and Event Management as part of the UNM educational leadership program. He currently volunteers to teach dual enrollment courses at To'hajiilee Community School as part of New Mexico State University in Grants. He also serves as coordinator for Rising Eagles Dual Enrollment (REDE) programs and several UNM Native leadership cohorts including the Native American Leadership in Doctoral Education (NALE); Promoting Our Leadership, Learning, and Empowering Our

Nations (POLLEN); American Indian Professional Educators Collaborative (AIPEC); and the Society of Native American Graduate Students at UNM (SNAGS). He also directs the Striking Eagle Native American Invitational (SENAI), which is one of the largest Native high school events that bridges athletics with a dual enrollment academy at UNM.

Michael Thompson (Mvskoke Creek) was born in Holdenville, Oklahoma, and raised on a cattle farm near the Flint River in southwest Georgia. He has been a teacher, writer, and occasional community activist in Georgia, Kansas, California, and New Mexico. He is married to Tina Deschenie (Diné/Hopi), and they have four children and several grandchildren. Most of his life he taught high school English, including fourteen years at Bloomfield High School, in Bloomfield, New Mexico. From 2014 until he retired in 2019, he served as the coordinator of alternative licensure at San Juan College (SJC) and as the site director of the Bisti Writing Project and represented SJC on the Navajo Nation Teacher Education Consortium. He has presented workshops on contemporary Native literature at state and national conferences and published poetry and articles in a variety of publications. Most recently he was a contributor to *The Diné Reader* (University of Arizona Press, 2021). He and his family support numerous Native American activities and political causes.

Pedro "Pete" Vallejo, EdD, is of Diné (Chíshí Diné clan) and Mexican-American descent. He received his EdD from the University of New Mexico in educational leadership. He is currently the principal of Pecos High School in Pecos, New Mexico. His academic interests lie in culturally responsive leadership in Indigenous and Hispanic education as well as issues that impact Indigenous and bilingual education. He has over twenty-six years of teaching and administrative experience working with all levels of K–12 in California and New Mexico. He also has experience working with postsecondary institutions, including New Mexico Highlands University, in educational leadership.

Christine B. Vining, PhD, CCC-SLP, is a bilingual Navajo speech-language pathologist at the University of New Mexico Center for Development and Disability (CDD) housed in the Health Sciences Center's Department of Pediatrics. Currently, she provides clinical services, training, and technical assistance to support individuals with autism spectrum disorder and their families through the Autism and Other Developmental Disabilities Division. She is a faculty member in the NM Leadership Education in Neurodevelopmental and Related Disabilities (LEND) program at the CDD representing the speech-language pathology profession.

Vincent Werito is Ta'neeszahnii (Tangle Clan), born for Naakai Dine'é (Traveler's Band clan). His maternal grandfathers are Kinłichiinii (Red House clan) and his paternal grandfathers are Tódichiinii (Bitter Water clan). He is originally from Na'neelzhiin (Torreon, New Mexico), a rural Navajo community southwest of Cuba, New Mexico. Werito is an associate professor in the College of Education and Health Sciences at the University of New Mexico in the Department of Language, Literacy, and Sociocultural Studies. His research examines the experiences of Indigenous youth in education, identifying exemplary practices in the education of Indigenous youth and using community-engaged approaches to create research partnerships, community-defined understandings of well-being, and successful aging with a health research focus. Currently, he serves as principal investigator (PI) and co-PI on several research studies and grants related to Indigenous community–engaged research and Diné language revitalization. He teaches the graduate and undergraduate courses American Indian (Indigenous) Education, Bilingual Education, and Educational Thought and Sociocultural Studies. Some of his recent publications focus on reclaiming Indigenous pedagogies, Navajo language advocacy, and using a Diné-centered politics to engage in community partnerships and research. He continues to work with schools in New Mexico and abroad to develop culture- and place-based culturally responsive education for Indigenous youth as well as working with Indigenous communities in their language revitalization efforts.

Duane "Chili" Yazzie is Diné from Shiprock, Navajo Nation. He has served his Shiprock community and the Navajo Nation for forty-five years. His credentials include being a grandpa, farmer, earth defender, and community leader. His life has been one of activism, and he has advocated for Indigenous civil and human rights. Chili is greatly concerned with the health of our Earth Mother and the kind of world we leave our children.

INDEX